BASIC PATTERNS
OF Chinese Grammar

D0017363

A Student's Guide to
Correct Structures
and Common Errors

Qin Xue Herzberg & Larry Herzberg

Stone Bridge Press • *Berkeley, California*

Published by
Stone Bridge Press
P.O. Box 8208
Berkeley, CA 94707
TEL 510-524-8732 • sbp@stonebridge.com • www.stonebridge.com

The publisher acknowledges with gratitude SIL International and its
development of Gentium Basic, http://scripts.sil.org/Gentium.

©2011 Qin Xue Herzberg and Larry Herzberg.

Printed in the United States of America.

2015   10 9 8 7 6 5 4

LIBRARY OF CONGRESS CATALOGING-IN-PUBLICATION DATA
(on file)

Contents

32 CHAPTER THREE
Nouns

39 CHAPTER FOUR
Verbs

112 CHAPTER TWELVE
Word-Choice Issues with Adverbs

INTRODUCTION

- -

Never Translate Literally, WORD-FOR-WORD! Translate the Gist of What's Being Said

If you learn nothing else from this book, learn the cardinal rule of translation from English into Chinese, or from any language into another: Never translate literally, word-for-word! This is especially true for slang expressions! Translating literally will result in faulty communication, or, as in so many cases, be really funny! Instead, always translate the basic idea, the gist of what's being said.

The two of us are professors of Chinese language at an excellent college in the Midwest, where we've taught for many years. Larry, a native English speaker, has taught Chinese for three decades at the college level. Xue Qin, his wife, a native speaker of Chinese and a graduate of Beijing Normal University in Chinese Language and Literature, has been doing her best to get college students and adult learners in the U.S. to learn her language for the past two decades. In spite of having been blessed with an incredible number of talented and motivated students over the years, we could fill a whole book with examples of our students violating the cardinal rule of translation and coming up with some hilarious as well as some really awful "no-no's" in their homework, essays, and tests.

Here are but a few prime examples of how our beloved students have, on occasion, butchered the most commonly spoken language on the planet. The "Correct Chinese" is labeled "*CC*"; the "Butchered Chinese" is "*BC.*"

My father is Chinese.

✔ *CC: Wǒ fùqin shì Zhōngguó rén.*
我父亲是中国人。

✘ *BC: Wǒ fùqin shì Zhōngguó.*
我父亲是中国。
Literally: My Dad is China!

I got it!—meaning "I understand"

✔ *CC: Wǒ míngbai le.*
我明白了。

✘ *BC: Wǒ dédào le.*
我得到了。
Literally: I obtained it!

We have dinner at home.

✔ *CC: Wǒmen zài jiāli chī wǎnfàn.*
我们在家里吃晚饭。
Literally: We at home eat dinner.

✘ *BC: Wǒmen yǒu wǎnfàn zài jiāli.*
我们有晚饭在家里。
Literally: We have/possess dinner at home.

The basic word order of Chinese is: Who, Where, What. The basic word order of English is: Who, What, Where.

I have a headache.

✔ *CC: Wǒ tóu téng.*
我头疼。

✘ *BC: Wǒ yǒu tóuténg.*
我有头疼。
(A literal translation.)

I have a cold.

✔ *CC: Wǒ gǎnmào le.*
我感冒了。

✘ *BC: Wǒ yǒu gǎnmào.*
我有感冒。
(A literal translation.)

The weather is cool.

✔ *CC: Tiānqi hěn liángkuài*。
天气很凉快 。

✘ *BC: Tiānqi hěn shuài.*
天气很帅。

NOTE: *Shuài* 帅 refers to men who are "cool" in the sense of handsome, smart-looking, debonair.

That guy is cool.

✔ *CC: Nàge rén hěn shuài.*
那个人很帅。

✘ *BC: Nàge rén hěn liángkuài.*
那个人很凉快。
That guy is cool (in temperature).

That car is really cool.

✔ *CC: Nàliàng chē zhēn kù!*
那辆车真酷!

✘ *BC: Nàliàng chē zhēn liángkuài.*
那辆车真凉快。
That car is really cool in temperature inside.

NOTE: *Kù* 酷 comes from "cool" in English.

I am going to the airport to pick up my friend.

✔ *CC: Wǒ dào fēijīchǎng qù jiē wǒde péngyou.*
我到飞机场去接我的朋友。

✖ *BC: Wǒ dào fēijīchǎng qù bǎ wǒde péngyou náqǐlái.*
我到飞机场去把我的朋友拿起来。
I am going to the airport to pick up my friend, in my hand, just like King Kong might!

I am going to the bank to pick up some money.
✔ *CC: Wǒ dào yínháng qù qǔ qián.*
我到银行去取钱。

✖ *BC: Wǒ dào yínháng qù náqǐ qián lái.*
我到银行去拿起钱来。
I'm going to the bank to grab some money and raise it up off the counter!

We trust that you will learn a lot more from our little book than simply to not translate literally. We have done our best to provide a handy reference tool for you to use when translating from English into Chinese. This is intended to supplement your Chinese language textbooks, not to replace them. We have addressed most of the major stumbling blocks faced by students at the beginning and intermediate levels of Mandarin Chinese language study, the ones that trouble our students through all four levels of college.

We divided the entries into various rather conventional topics, such as parts of speech (nouns, verbs, adjectives, conjunctions) as well as into basic topics, such as word order, time expressions, even letter writing.

One persistent difficulty is word choice when translating verbs from English into Chinese. While English is more precise when it comes to nouns and adjectives, the Chinese tend to be more precise in their use of verbs. For example, they have five ways to translate the verb "to tell," depending on whether one is telling a story, telling something to someone (informing), telling someone to do something, and so on.

Our intent is for this reference guide to assist you with your homework, to save your teachers countless numbers of red pens, and to save you from having your beautiful work all marked up. More importantly, of course, we hope this gently guides you to avoid most of the basic mistakes non-native speakers make when speaking or writing Chinese. Use this reference guide judiciously, and you'll leave *BC* (Butchered Chinese) behind and speak only *CC* (Correct Chinese). Enjoy!

Qin Xue and Larry Herzberg
Professors of Chinese
Calvin College
Grand Rapids, Michigan

CHAPTER ONE

. . . .

WORD ORDER

(1) Basic word order

The basic word order in English is Who, What, Where, When. The basic word order in Chinese is Who, When, Where, What.

> English: We ate lunch at McDonald's at 1:00 yesterday afternoon.
> Chinese: We yesterday afternoon at 1:00 at McDonald's ate lunch.
> *Wǒmen zuótiān xiàwǔ yìdiǎn zhōng zài Màidāngláo chīle wǔfàn.*
> 我们昨天下午一点钟在麦当劳 吃了午饭。

> English: We saw a Chinese movie at that movie theater Saturday evening.
> Chinese: We Saturday evening at that movie theater saw a Chinese movie.
> *Wǒmen xīngqīliù wǎnshang zài nàge diànyǐngyuàn kànle yíge Zhōngguó diànyǐng.*
> 我们星期六晚上在那个电影院看了一个中国电影。

(2) Action and location: someone does something somewhere

English: Who, what, where, (when)
Chinese: Who, (when) where, what

English: I eat dinner at home.
Chinese: I at home eat dinner .
Wǒ zài jiāli chī wǎnfàn.
我在家里吃晚饭。

English: I study in the library.
Chinese: I at the library study.
Wǒ zài túshūguǎn niànshū.
我在图书馆念书。

(3) Action and time: when somebody does something

English: Who, what, (where) when
Chinese: Who, when, (where) what

The time WHEN something happens always comes before the verb.

English: I get up at 8:00.
Chinese: I at 8:00 get up.
Wǒ bādiǎn zhōng qǐchuáng.
我八点钟起床。

English: I eat breakfast at 8:30.
Chinese: I at 8:30 eat breakfast.
Wǒ bādiǎn bàn chī zǎofàn.
我八点半吃早饭。

(4) Word order for expressing WHEN something happened

The biggest, most general time words come first in Chinese:

> English: day, month, year
> Chinese: year, month, day

> English: Saturday, October 1, 1949 (Founding of the PRC)
> Chinese: 1949, October 1, Saturday
> *Yījiǔsìjiǔnián, shíyuè yíhào, xīngqīliù*
> 1949年10月1日，星期六。

> English: 8:00 a.m. on July 4, 1820 (America's First Independence day)
> Chinese: 1820, July 4, at 8:00 a.m.
> *Yībāèrlíngnián qīyuè sìhào, zǎoshang bādiǎn zhōng.*
> 1820年7月4日，早上八点钟。

(5) Word order for duration of time: how long someone did something

The word order for expressing the length or duration of time is very different from expressing the time when an action occurred. Here, the length of time of an action can come at the end of the sentence, whereas this can NEVER happen with expressing WHEN something occurred.

> I slept eight hours of sleep.
> *Wǒ shuìle bāge zhōngtou (xiǎoshí) de jiào.*
> 我睡了八个钟头 (小时) 的觉。

OR, if you are stating the length of time you spent on various activities, in addition to sleeping:

I slept (for) eight hours.
In terms of my sleeping, I slept eight hours.
Wǒ shuìjiào shuìle bāge zhōngtou (xiǎoshí).
我睡觉睡了八个钟头 (小时) 。

Once you've established sleeping as your topic of conversation, then you can, of course, simply say, as we would in English:

I slept eight hours.
Wǒ shuìle bāge zhōngtou (xiǎoshí).
我睡了八个钟头 (小时) 。

Yesterday, I studied for five hours.
Yesterday, I studied five hours of books.
Zuótiān wǒ niànle wǔge zhōngtou (xiǎoshí) de shū.
昨天我念了五个钟头 (小时) 的书。

OR, if you're enumerating the relative amount of time you spent doing various things yesterday:

I studied for five hours yesterday.
Yesterday as for my studying, I studied (for) five hours.
Zuótiān wǒ niànshū niànle wǔge zhōngtou (xiǎoshí).
昨天我念书念了五个钟头 (小时) 。

And once we've established "studying" as the topic of discussion, then we can simply say, as in English:

I studied (for) five hours.
Wǒ niànle wǔge zhōngtou (xiǎoshí).
我念了五个钟头 (小时) 。

HOWEVER, when a length of time is given in a sentence with negation, *bù* 不 or *méi/méiyǒu* 没/没有 , then the period of time comes BEFORE the verb:

English: I haven't slept for two days.
Chinese: I for two days have not slept.
✔ *CC: Wǒ liǎngtiān méi shuìjiào le.*
我两天没睡觉了。

✘ *BC: Wǒ méi shuìjiào liǎngtiān.*
我没睡觉两天。
Literally: I haven't slept two days.

English: I haven't smoked for a year.
Chinese: I for one year have not smoked.
CC: Wǒ yìnián méi xīyān le.
我一年没吸烟了。

(6) Placement of "why" in a question

The word "why?" *wèishénme* 为什么, is always placed AFTER the subject of the sentence, not before as it is in English (unless the speaker is being particularly emphatic and almost indignant!):

English: Why are you studying Chinese?
Chinese: You why (for what reason) are studying Chinese?
✔ *CC: Nǐ wèishénme xué zhōngwén?*
你为什么学中文？

English: Why didn't she come to class?
Chinese: She why (for what reason) didn't come to class?
✔ *CC: Tā wèishénme méi shàngkè?*
她为什么没上课？

✘ *BC: Wèishénme tā méi shàngkè?*
为什么她没上课？
Why in the world didn't she come to class?!

CHAPTER TWO

· ·

TIME EXPRESSIONS

(1) Expressing simultaneous actions

To express two simultaneous actions, as in "When . . . " or "While . . . ," use *shíhou* 时候. In English, the "when/while" clause can either begin the sentence or be placed in the subordinate clause. In English, one says either "When Chinese people eat, they use chopsticks" or "Chinese people use chopsticks when they eat."

In Chinese, the "when/while" clause must come first:

> English: She listens to music when she takes a walk.
> Chinese: Her walking times (she) listens to music.
> *Tā sànbù de shíhou tīng yīnyuè.*
> 她散步的时候听音乐。

> English: They watch TV when (while) they eat dinner.
> Chinese: When (while) they eat dinner, they watch TV.
> *Tāmen chī wǎnfàn de shíhou kàn diànshì.*
> 他们吃晚饭的时候看电视。

HOWEVER, if by "when" you mean "after . . . ," then "when . . . "

is translated as *yǐhòu* 以后:

> When (after) I graduate, I'm going to China to teach English.

✔ *CC: Wǒ bìle yè yǐhòu dào Zhōngguó qù jiāo Yīngyǔ.*
我毕了业以后到中国去教英语。

✘ *BC: Wǒ bìyè de shíhou dào Zhōngguó qù jiāo Yīngyǔ.*
我毕业的时候到中国去教英语。
> When I'm graduating, just as I'm walking up to get my diploma, I'm already on my way to China! (Is the graduation hall on the way, or am I grabbing my diploma as I get on the plane?!)

✘ *BC: Yǐhòu wǒ bìyèle dào Zhōngguó qù jiāo Yīngyǔ.*
以后我毕业了到中国去教英语。

That's because 以后 and 以前 never come BEFORE what they refer to!

(2) To say "again": *zài* 再 vs. *yòu* 又

When you say that someone will do something again in the future, use *zài* 再:

> I will go to China again next year.
> *Wǒ míngnián huì zài dào Zhōngguó qù.*
> 我明年会再到中国去。

> We're going to see that movie again tomorrow evening.
> *Wǒmen míngtiān wǎnshang huì zài kàn nèige diànyǐng.*
> 我们明天晚上会再看那个电影。

When you say something happened again in the past, use *yòu* 又:

> I went to China again last year.
> *Wǒ qùnián yòu dào Zhōngguó qù le.*
> 我去年又到中国去了。

We saw that movie again last night.
Wǒmen zuótiān wǎnshang yòu kàn le nèige diànyǐng.
我们昨天晚上又看了那个电影。

HOWEVER, be aware that before certain helping verbs, such as *shì* 是 (am, is, are), *xiǎng* 想 (think), *néng* 能 (can/able to), *yào* 要 (want), *yǐhòu* 以后 (after), and *huì* 会 (can/know), you can only use *yòu* 又 (again, regardless of tense):

Tomorrow there's going to be a test again.
Míngtiān yòu shì yíge kǎoshì.
明天又是一个考试。

They need to/want to see the doctor yet again this afternoon.
Tāmen jīntiān xiàwǔ yòu yào qù kàn dàifu.
他们今天下午又要去看大夫。

(3) "After"/"later": *yǐhòu* 以后 vs. *ránhòu* 然后

When you say that someone will do something and then afterward/later will do something else in the future, or that someone generally does something and then afterward/later does something else, you can either use *yǐhòu* 以后 or *ránhòu* 然后 for "after that"/"afterward"/"later."

HOWEVER, depending on which of the two expressions you use, the structure of the sentence will be different:

After she goes to class, she'll go work.
Tā xià le kè yǐhòu jiù huì qù gōngzuò.
她下了课以后就会去工作。

OR:

She's in class right now, and afterward will go work.
Tā xiànzài zhèngzài shàngkè, ránhòu tā huì qù gōngzuò.
她现在正在上课, 然后她会去工作。

You cannot use *hòulái* 后来, which is only used for actions in the past.

✘ *BC: Tā xiànzài zhèngzài shàngkè, hòulái tā huì qù gōngzuò.*
她现在正在上课, 后来她会去工作。

Every evening they watch TV, and after that they go to bed.
✔ *CC: Tāmen měitiān wǎnshang kànle diànshì yǐhòu jiù shàngchuáng.*
他们每天晚上看了电视以后就上床。

了 is used here because you're really saying: "Having watched TV, they then go to bed."

OR:

✔ *CC: Tāmen měitiān wǎnshang kàn diànshì, ránhòu jiù shàngchuáng.*
他们每天晚上看电视, 然后就上床。

了 is NOT used here because you're saying: "They watch TV, and after that they go to bed.

✘ *BC: Tāmen měitiān wǎnshang kàn diànshì, hòulái jiù shàngchuáng.*
他们每天晚上看电视, 后来就上床。

HOWEVER, there is a difference between the use of *yǐhòu* 以后 and *ránhòu* 然后. *Ránhòu* 然后 always implies that one action logically or naturally follows the other, whereas *yǐhòu* 以后 can be used even with two actions that are not necessarily a logical or natural sequence. As a result, *ránhòu* 然后 cannot be used with a negative clause:

> He's working at a factory this year, but afterward he
> doesn't plan to work there any more.
> ✔ *CC: Tā jīnnián zài gōngchǎnglǐ gōngzuò, kěshì yǐhòu tā
> bùdǎsuan zài nèr gōngzuò le.*
> 他今年在工厂里工作，可是以后他不打算在那儿工作
> 了。
>
> ✘ *BC: Tā jīnnián zài gōngchǎnglǐ gōngzuò, kěshì ránhòu tā
> bùdǎsuan zài nèr gōngzuò le.*
> 他今年在工厂里工作，可是然后他不打算在那儿工作
> 了。

The use of *hòulái* 后来 vs. *ránhòu* 然后

When you say that someone did something in the past and after
that or later did something else, or that someone regularly did
something in the past and after that or later did something else,
use either *hòulái* 后来 or *ránhòu* 然后. Unlike *yǐhòu* 以后, neither
can be used after the verb in the first clause, but must be placed
at the beginning of the second clause.

> Mr. Wang taught Chinese in college for twenty years,
> and after that retired.
> ✔ *CC: Wáng Xiānsheng zài dàxué jiāole èrshíniánde Hànyǔ,
> hòulái jiù tuìxiū le.*
> 王先生在大学教了二十年的汉语，后来就退休了。
>
> ✘ *BC: Wáng Xiānsheng zài dàxué jiāole èrshíniánde Hànyǔ,
> ránhòu jiù tuìxiū le.*
> 王先生在大学教了二十年的汉语，然后就退休了。

This is *BC* unless you mean that it logically follows that after
teaching anything for twenty years, everyone retires—by law or
custom, etc.

They dated for over two years, and afterward they got married.

✔ *CC: Tāmen tánle liǎngniánduō de lián-ài, hòulái jiù jiéhūn le.*
他们谈了两年多的恋爱，后来就结婚了。

✘ *BC: Tāmen tánle liǎngniánduō de lián-ài, ránhòu jiù jiéhūn le.*
他们谈了两年多的恋爱，然后就结婚了。

This is *BC* unless you assume that dating always logically ends in marriage, which we know is painfully not the case!

HOWEVER, just as when it's used in the future tense, *ránhòu* 然后 cannot be used with a negative clause with the past tense either, since *ránhòu* 然后 always implies a logical sequence of events.

My father smoked for twenty years, but afterward he didn't smoke any more.

✔ *CC: Wǒ fùqin chōule èrshínián de yān, kěshì hòulái tā bùchōu le.*
我父亲抽了二十年的烟，可是后来他不抽了。

✘ *BC: Wǒ fùqin chōule èrshínián de yān, kěshì ránhòu tā bùchōu le.*
我父亲抽了二十年的烟，可是然后他不抽了。

Finally, no matter what the tense, you can always use *yǐhòu* 以后 after the verb in the first clause to mean "after" doing something or someone did, does, or will do something else:

After she goes to class, she'll go to work.
Tā xià le kè yǐhòu jiù huì qù gōngzuò.
她下了课以后就会去工作。

Every evening after they watch TV, they go to bed.
Tāmen měitiān wǎnshang kànle diànshì yǐhòu jiù shàngchuáng.
他们每天晚上看了电视以后就上床。

After she went to class, she went to work.
Tā xiàle kè yǐhòu jiù qù gōngzuò le.
她下了课以后就去工作了。

Every evening after they watched TV, they went to bed.
Tāmen měitiān wǎnshang kànle diànshì yǐhòu jiù shàngchuáng le.
他们每天晚上看了电视以后就上床了。

In NONE of the four examples above would you use *ránhòu* 然后 using the same sentence structure.

After eating dinner, they want to go see a movie.

✔ CC: *Chīle wǎnfàn yǐhòu, tāmen jiù yào qù kàn diànyǐng .*
吃了晚饭以后，他们就要去看电影。

✘ BC: *Chīle wǎnfàn ránhòu, tāmen jiù yào qù kàn diànyǐng.*
吃了晚饭然后，他们就要去看电影。

(4) "Last week, this week, next week" and "last month, this month, next month" follow the same pattern, with *shàng* 上 indicating "last . . . ," *zhè/zhèi* 这 indicating "this . . .," and *xià* 下 indicating "next . . ."

last week (month)
shàng(ge) xīngqī (yuè)
上 (个) 星期 (月)

this week (month)
zhèige xīngqī (yuè)
这个星期 (月)

next week (month)
xià(ge) xīngqī (yuè)
下 (个) 星期 (月)

HOWEVER, days (*tiān* 天) and years (*nián* 年), the smallest and
largest of the general time words, are expressed similarly to each
other but differently from weeks and months:

yesterday (last year)
zuótiān (qùnián)
昨天 (去年)

today (this year)
jīntiān (jīnnián)
今天 (今年)

tomorrow (next year)
míngtiān (míngnián)
明天 (明年)

CHAPTER THREE

. . . .

NOUNS

(1) Plurals in Chinese

Every noun in Chinese is both singular and plural:

书	*shū*	book or books
狗	*gǒu*	dog or dogs
人	*rén*	person or people

HOWEVER, there are a limited number of nouns referring to people that can take the suffix *men* 们 to clarify that they are plural. This very short list includes the following:

friends	*péngyoumen*	朋友们
children	*háizimen*	孩子们
students	*xuéshengmen*	学生们

(2) When counting things, measure words must always be used between the number and the noun

one person	*yíge rén*	一个人
two cats	*liǎngzhī māo*	两只猫
three books	*sānběn shū*	三本书

Measure words must also be used between "this" or "that" and a noun:

this cat	*zhèizhī māo*	这只猫
that book	*nèiběn shū*	那本书

(3) This and that

This book	*zhèi (zhè) běn shū*	这本书
That book	*nèi (nà) běn shū*	那本书

These books	*zhèixie (zhèxie) shū*	这些书
Those books	*nèixiē (nàxie) shū*	那些书

These four books	*zhèi (zhè) sìběn shū*	这四本书
Those four books	*nèi (nà) sìběn shū*	那四本书

(4) Nouns for nationalities and languages

Correct usage for "China," *Zhōngguó* 中国, and "Chinese language," *zhōngwén* 中文:

Chinese = Zhōngguó 中国, when "Chinese" is an
    adjective that precedes a noun
Chinese = *Zhōngguó rén* 中国人, when "Chinese" refers to
    Chinese person/people
Chinese = *Zhōngwén* 中文 or *Hànyǔ* 汉语, when "Chinese"
    refers to the language

I have a Chinese pen.
Wǒ yǒu Zhōngguó bǐ.
我有中国笔。

My wife is Chinese.
Wǒ tàitai shì Zhōngguó rén.
我太太是中国人。

My wife teaches Chinese.
Wǒ tàitai jiāo Zhōngwén (Hànyǔ).
我太太教中文 (汉语) 。

The same rules apply for all nationalities and languages.

(5) All (of some noun): *dōu* 都 vs. *suǒyǒude* 所有的

The word *dōu* 都 (both/all) always follows the noun to which it
refers; *dōu* 都 can NEVER precede a noun!

If you use *suǒyǒude* 所有的 for emphasis, it comes before the
noun to which it refers; but you still need to put *dōu* 都 after that
noun:

All children like candy.
Háizi dōu xǐhuān táng.
孩子都喜欢糖。

OR, for emphasis:

✔ *CC: Suǒyǒude háizi dōu xǐhuān táng.*
所有的孩子都喜欢糖。

✖ *BC: Dōu háizi xǐhuān táng.*
都孩子喜欢糖。
Literally: All children like candy. (BUT *dōu* can NEVER precede a noun!)

I like all (or both) those children.
Nèixie háizi wǒ dōu xǐhuān.
那些孩子我都喜欢。

OR, for emphasis:

Suǒyǒude nèixie háizi wǒ dōu xǐhuān.
所有的那些孩子我都喜欢。

(6) How to express the indefinites

Everyone, everything, everywhere, no one, nothing, nowhere:

Everything's delicious.
Shénme dōu hǎochī.
什么都好吃。

Everywhere is noisy.
Nǎr (shénme dìfang) dōu hěn chǎo.
哪儿 (什么地方) 都很吵。

Nothing is delicious.
Shénme dōu bù hǎochī.
什么都不好吃。

Nowhere is quiet.
Nǎr (shénme dìfang) dōu bù ānjìng.
哪儿 (什么地方) 都不安静。

Whatever, whoever, wherever:

I'll have (drink) whatever you're having.
Nǐ hē shénme, wǒ jiù hē shénme.
你喝什么，我就喝什么。
Literally: You drink what(ever), I'll (then) drink
what(ever).

Whoever you like, I'll like.
Nǐ xǐhuān shéi, wǒ jiù xǐhuān shéi.
你喜欢谁，我就喜欢谁。
Literally: You like who(ever), I'll (then) like who(ever).

I'll go wherever you go.
Nǐ dào nǎr qù, wǒ jiù dào nǎr qù.
你到哪儿去，我就到哪儿去。
Literally: You go where (wherever), I'll (then) go where
(wherever).

(7) How to express not even one bit of something

I don't have any ____.
Wǒ yìdiǎn(r) ____ yě (or dōu) méiyǒu.
我一点儿......也 (都) 没有。

I don't want any ____.
Wǒ yìdiǎn(r) ____ yě (dōu) búyào.
我一点儿...也 (都) 不要。

I don't have any money (at all).
Wǒ yìdiǎn(r) qián yě (dōu) méiyǒu.
我一点 (儿) 钱也 (都) 没有。

I don't want any beer (at all).
Wǒ yìdiǎn(r) píjiǔ yě (dōu) búyào.
我一点 (儿) 啤酒也 (都) 不要。

HOWEVER, for things that you can quantify/count, as in "I don't even have one ____," use *wǒ yíge* 我一个 (or appropriate measure word) *yě (dōu) méiyǒu* 也 (都) 没有:

I don't even have one friend.
Wǒ yíge péngyou yě méiyǒu.
我一个朋友也没有。

I don't even want one ____.
Wǒ yíge (or appropriate measure word) *yě (dōu) búyào.*
我一个 ... 也 (都) 不要。

I don't even want one hamburger.
Wǒ yíge hànbǎobāo yě búyào.
我一个汉堡包也不要。

I don't even have one dollar.
Wǒ yíkuài qián yě (dōu) méiyǒu.
我一块钱也 (都) 没有。

I don't even want one Japanese book.
Wǒ yìběn Rìwén shū yě (or *dōu*) *búyào.*
我一本日文 书也 (都) 不要。

(8) Location words

Relative location words come after the place or object, not before, as in English:

> on the table
> *zhuōzi shàng(tou)*
> 桌子上 (头)
> Literally: table on/table top

> in the store
> *shāngdiàn lǐ(tou)*
> 商店里 (头)
> Literally: store('s) inside

BUT, never use *lǐ(tou)* 里 (头) after the name of a country or city:

> Her home is in China.
> ✔ *CC: Tā jiā zài Zhōngguó.*
> 她家在中国。

> ✘ *BC: Tā jiā zài Zhōngguó lǐ(tou).*
> 她家在中国里 (头) 。

CHAPTER FOUR

· ·

VERBS

(1) Past tense

For action verbs, from eating and sleeping to walking, running, or even studying: add *le* 了:

> I went.
> *Wǒ qù le.*
> 我去了。

> I ate.
> *Wǒ chīfàn le.*
> 我吃饭了。

> I slept.
> *Wǒ shuìjiào le.*
> 我睡觉了。

Non-action verbs (feelings) are no different from present tense; don't add *le* 了.

Non-action verbs of thought, feeling, and emotion, and verbs of knowing and informing include everything from "like" and "love" to "think," "feel," "understand," "know," "ask," "tell," etc.:

> I liked him.
> ✔ *CC: Wǒ xǐhuān tā.*
> 我喜欢他。
>
> ✘ *BC: Wǒ xǐhuān tā le.*
> 我喜欢他了。
> I came to like him.
>
> Ten years ago I liked white clothing.
> ✔ *CC: Wǒ shíniánqián xǐhuān báisède yīfu.*
> 我十年前喜欢白色的衣服。
>
> ✘ *BC: Wǒ shíniánqián xǐhuān le báisède yīfu.*
> 我十年前喜欢了白色的衣服。
>
> I loved her.
> *Wǒ ài tā.*
> 我爱她。
>
> I wanted to buy it.
> *Wǒ yào mǎi.*
> 我要买。

Non-action verbs used to express asking or telling are exceptions to this rule IF they have a simple direct object:

> I asked her something.
> *Wǒ wèn le tā yíjiàn shì.*
> 我问了她一件事。

BUT:

Yesterday I asked her if she wanted to go shopping with me today.
Zuótiān wǒ wèn tā xiǎng bùxiǎng jīntiān hé wǒ yìqǐ qù mǎi dōngxi.
昨天我问她想不想今天和我一起去买东西。

(2) Present tense

For the plain present tense, use the dictionary form of the verb:

She reads/is reading a book.
Tā kànshū.
她看书。

He watches/is watching TV.
Tā kàn diànshì.
他看电视。

To emphasize doing something right now, either put *zài* 在 in front of the verb:

She is reading a book (right now).
Tā zài kànshū.
她在看书。

OR: Put *ne* 呢 after the verb:

Tā kànshū ne.
她看书呢。

OR: Put *zài* 在 in front of the verb and *ne* 呢 after it:

Tā zài kànshū ne.
她在看书呢。

OR: Put *zhe* 着 after the verb:

> *Tā kànzhe shū.*
> 她看着书。

OR: Put *zhe* 着 after the verb and *ne* 呢 after it:

> *Tā kànzhe shū ne.*
> 她看着书呢。

(3) Future tense

The present tense of ALL verbs can be used to express future tense as well:

> I drink coffee every day.
> *Wǒ měitiān hē kāfēi.*
> 我每天喝咖啡。

> I will drink coffee tomorrow.
> *Wǒ míngtiān hē kāfēi.*
> 我明天喝咖啡。

BUT, to emphasize future tense, put either *yào* 要 or *huì* 会 in front of the verb. *Yào* 要 implies "want to" and therefore "will"; *huì* 会 implies "able to" and therefore "will":

> They will go to China next year [in the sense that they want to and therefore will].
> *Tāmen míngnián yào dào Zhōngguó qù.*
> 他们明年要到中国去。

They will go to China next year [in the sense that they have the money, the time, etc. to able to go, and so "will go"].
Tāmen míngnián huì dào Zhōngguó qù.
他们明年会到中国去。

(4) The word "it" is usually implied by the verb

Unlike in English, the word "it" is rarely used in Chinese but is implied by the verb:

I saw it.
Wǒ kànjiàn le.
我看见了。

I bought it.
Wǒ mǎi le.
我买了。

You cannot use "it," *tā* 它, to refer to the date or time:

It's Friday (today).
✔ *CC: Jīntiān shì xīngqīwǔ.*
今天是星期五。
(NOTE: in Chinese, the word "today" is needed.)

✖ *BC: Tā shì xīngqīwǔ jīntiān.*
它是星期五今天。

It's the first of June (today).
✔ *CC: Jīntiān shì liùyuè yíhào.*
今天是六月一号。

✖ *BC: Tā shì liùyuè yíhào jīntiān.*
它是六月一号今天。

You cannot use *tā* 它 to refer to the weather:

It's raining.
✔ *CC: Xiàyǔ le.*
下雨了。

✖ *BC: Tā xiàyǔ.*
它下雨。
Literally: It is raining.

You cannot use *tā* 它 in sentences like "It's mine" or "It's his." Instead use "this" *zhè* 这 or "that" *nà* 那:

It's mine.
Zhè (nà) shì wǒde.
这 (那)是我的。

You cannot use *tā* 它 when referring to an abstract thing or event:

It's a good idea.
Nà shì yíge hǎo zhǔyi.
那是一个好主意。

It doesn't matter.
Méiyǒu guānxi.
没有关系。

It's very hard to talk with him.
Hěn nán gēn tā duìhuà.
很难跟他对话。

This is equally true when "it" is used as a direct object to refer to abstract things:

Maybe he has been reformed, but I doubt it.
Yěxǔ tā gǎiguò zìxīn le, dànshi wǒ hěn huáiyí.
也许他改过自新了，但是我很怀疑。

You cannot use *tā* 它 when stating who someone is, in sentences like "It's me" or "It's Mary":

> It's me.
> ✔ *CC: Shì wǒ.*
> 是我。

> ✘ *BC: Tā shì wǒ.*
> 它是我。

You cannot use *tā* 它 when "it" is used in English to refer to human beings, like a child:

> This is a rite of passage that every child has to go through as it grows up.
> *Zhè shì měi yíge háizi zài chéngzhǎng guòchéng zhōng bìxū jīngguò de.*
> 这是每一个孩子在成长过程中必须经过的。

If you use "it" as a direct object referring to a place, you cannot use *tā* 它. Instead use *zhèlǐ* 这里 or *nàlǐ* 那里:

> I like it here.
> *Wǒ xǐhuān zhèlǐ.*
> 我喜欢这里。

There are only two cases where "it" in English can be translated as *tā* 它 in Chinese:

(a) *Tā* 它 can be used to refer to animals

> There is a cat over there. It has black fur.
> *Nàbiān yǒu yìzhī māo. Tā yǒu hēisède máo.*
> 那边有一只猫。它有黑色的毛。

(b) *Tā* 它 can be used for direct objects with the *bǎ* 把 pattern

---

"Where is my book?" "I put it on the table."
"Wǒde shū zai nǎlǐ?" "Wǒ bǎ tā fàngzài zhuōzi shàng le."
"我的书在哪里?" "我把它放在桌子上了。"

When the *bǎ* 把 pattern is not used, however, you cannot use *tā* 它 to refer to the direct object:

a room without furniture in it
yíge méiyǒu jiāju de fángjiān
一个没有家具的房间

(5) Helping verbs (prepositions in English)

(a) *Gěi* 给, meaning "to give," also functions as a helping verb

---

Gei 给 can mean "to do something for someone":

I cooked dinner for my friends.
Wǒ gěi wǒde péngyou zuò le wǎnfàn.
我给我的朋友做了晚饭

Gěi 给 is used in communication (phone calls, letters, etc.) to indicate the person to whom the communication is sent:

I phoned (to) my mother.
Wǒ gěi wǒ mǔqin dǎ le diànhuà.
我给我母亲打了电话。

I wrote a letter to my mother.
Wǒ gěi wǒ mǔqin xiě le yìfēng xìn.
我给我母亲写了一封信。

BUT, as the main verb, gěi 给 simply means "to give":

I give my little sister money.
Wǒ gěi wǒ mèimei qián.
我给我妹妹钱。

(b) *Gēn* 跟 by itself means "to follow," but as a helping verb, besides meaning "and" (see p. 73), most frequently *gēn* 跟 means "with"

to speak with/to someone
gēn . . . shuōhuà
跟 . . . 说话

to chat with someone
gēn . . . tántán
跟 . . . 谈谈

to discuss with someone
gēn . . . tǎolùn
跟 . . . 讨论

OR:

gēn . . . shāngliang
跟 . . . 商量

to argue with someone
gēn . . . zhēnglùn
跟 . . . 争论

to quarrel with someone
gēn ... chǎojià
跟 ... 吵架

to have connections with someone
gēn ... yǒu guānxi
跟 ... 有关系

BUT:

to be angry with someone
shēng (someone) *de qì*
生 ... 的气

I'm angry with my friend.
Wǒ shēng wǒ péngyou de qì.
我生我朋友的气。

I agree with you.
✔ *CC: Wǒ tóngyì nǐde yìjian.*
我同意你的意见。
✔ *CC: Wǒ tóngyì!*
我同意。

✘ *BC: Wǒ gēn nǐ tóngyì.*
我跟你同意。

AND: *Gēn* 跟 is used in many expressions where there is NO
preposition in English:

to marry someone
gēn ... jiéhūn
跟 ... 结婚

Who is she marrying?
Tā gēn shéi jiéhūn?
她跟谁结婚?
Literally: With whom is she marrying?

to divorce someone
gēn... líhūn
跟... 离婚

She divorced him last year.
Tā qùnián gēn tā líhūn le.
她去年跟他离婚了。
Literally: She with him divorced...

to greet someone
gēn... dǎ zhāohu
跟... 打招呼

That old gentleman just greeted me.
Nèiwèi lǎo xiānsheng gānggāng gēn wǒ dǎle zhāohu.
那位老先生刚刚跟我打了招呼。

(c) *Duì* 对 as a verb by itself means "to face." Therefore, as a helping verb, it has the idea of "vis-à-vis" or "concerning/in regard to." It can be translated as "toward," "to," "in," "as far as," "about," etc.

My parents are nice to me.
Wǒ(de) fùmǔ duì wǒ hěn hǎo.
我(的)父母对我很好。

She's very considerate of ("toward") her roommate.
Tā duì tāde tóngwū hěn tǐtiē.
她对她的同屋很体贴。

I'm very curious about ("concerning") her roommate.
Wǒ duì tāde tóngwū hěn hàoqí.
我对她的同屋很好奇。

I am interested in ("in regard to") sports.
Wǒ duì yùndòng gǎn (yǒu) xìngqu.
我对运动感(有)兴趣。

That career is appropriate for you.
Nèige zhíyè duì nǐ hěn héshì.
那个职业对你很合适。

Learning Chinese is beneficial for ("to") you.
Xué Hànyǔ duì nǐ yǒu hǎochù.
学汉语对你有好处。

As far as I'm concerned, that movie is boring.
Duì wǒ lái shuō, nàge diànyǐng méiyìsi.
对我来说，那个电影没意思。

(d) *Yòng* 用 by itself is a verb meaning "to use." But as a helping verb, *yòng* 用 has the idea of "using. . . ." It can be translated as "with" in the sense of "using something."

Chinese people eat with chopsticks.
Zhōngguó rén yòng kuàizi chīfàn.
中国人用筷子吃饭。

The teacher wrote the characters with a brush.
Lǎoshī yòng máobǐ xiě le nàxie zì.
老师用毛笔写了那些字。

BUT, *yòng* 用 can also be used to mean "in" when it has to do with speaking "in" (using) a certain language or paying "in" a certain currency:

She told him in Chinese.
Tā yòng Hànyǔ gàosu tā.
她用汉语告诉他。

He paid in RMB.
Tā yòng rénmínbì fù le qián.
他用人民币付了钱。

(e) Use *wèi* 为 to express "for (someone or something's sake)"

My parents sacrificed a lot for me.
Wǒ fùmǔ wèi wǒ zuòchū le hěn dàde xīshēng.
我父母为我做出了很大的牺牲。

My parents were proud of their son.
Wǒ fùmǔ wèi tāmen de érzi gǎndào jiāoào.
我父母为他们的儿子感到骄傲。

We celebrated my mother's birthday (for her sake).
Wǒmen wèi māma qìngzhù le tāde shēngrì.
我们为妈妈庆祝了她的生日。

I was concerned for my Mom (for her health, etc.).
Wǒ wèi wǒ māma dānxīn le.
我为我妈妈担心了。

(f) Use *tì* 替 to express "for" in the sense of "substituting for"; "in place of"

Mrs. Li taught for Mrs. Wang.
Lǐ tàitai tì Wáng tàitai jiāoshū le.
李太太替王太太教书了。

My daughter cooked for me last night.
Wǒde nǚer zuótiān wǎnshang tì wǒ zuòfàn le.
我的女儿昨天晚上替我做饭了。

(g) Use different translations of the preposition "for," depending on the meaning

To express "for" as in "for the sake of," use *wèi* 为:

> I cooked for Mom (in the sense of "for her sake"/"for her benefit").
> *Wǒ wèi Māma zuò le fàn.*
> 我为妈妈做了饭。

To express "for" as in "giving someone the favor of . . . ," use *gěi* 给:

> I cooked for Mom.
> *Wǒ gěi Māma zuò le fàn.*
> 我给妈妈做了饭。

To express "for" as in meaning "in place of" or "instead of," use *tì* 替:

> I cooked for Mom (substituting for her as our regular cook).
> *Wǒ tì Māma zuò le fàn*
> 我替妈妈做了饭。

(6) Going, coming, returning

To say "to go to someplace," use *dào* ___ *qù,* 到 . . . 去:

> I am going to China.
> *Wǒ dào Zhōngguó qù.*
> 我到中国去。

To say "to return to someplace," use *huídào*___*qù,* 回到 . . . 去:

I am returning home.
✔ CC: *Wǒ huídào jiālǐ qù.*
我回到家里去。

✖ *BC: Wǒ huíqù jiālǐ.*
我回去家里。

(7) The *bǎ* 把 pattern with verbs

The *bǎ* 把 pattern is used with verbs that are more than one syllable (i.e., verbs with a complement attached) to put the direct object in front of the verb:

She reads the newspaper every day.
Tā měitiān kàn bàozhǐ.
她每天看报纸。

BUT:

She put the newspaper on the table.
Tā bǎ bàozhǐ fàngzài zhuōzi shang.
她把报纸放在桌子上。

She picked up the chopsticks.
Tā bǎ kuàizi náqǐlái le.
她把筷子拿起来了。

Please open the door.
Qǐng bǎ mén dǎkāi.
请把门打开。

HOWEVER, the *bǎ* 把 pattern is also used with a verb that is a single syllable IF the direct object is some specific thing and not some general item:

He ate THE food.
Tā bǎ fàn chī le.
他把饭吃了。

BUT:

He ate (some) food.
Tā chīfàn le.
他吃饭了。

I gave those children THE candy.
Wǒ bǎ táng gěile nèixie háizi.
我把糖给了那些孩子。

I gave the children (some) candy.
Wǒ gěile nèixie háizi táng.
我给了那些孩子糖。

(8) The *shì . . . de* 是 . . . 的 pattern for past tense actions

Use the *shì . . . de* 是 . . . 的 pattern to emphasize when, how, or where something happened IN THE PAST, or who did it:

I came yesterday (not today).
Wǒ shì zuótiān lái de.
我是昨天来的。

I came by boat (not by plane).
Wǒ shì zuò chuán lái de.
我是坐船来的。

I was born in Beijing.
Wǒ shì zài Běijīng chūshēng de.
我是在北京出生的。

It was I who did it (not someone else).
Nà shì wǒ zuò de.
那是我做的。

(9) The different ways to express passive voice ("was . . . by . . .")

The Chinese do not use passive voice anywhere near as frequently as we do in English. Below are some occasions when you will, however, hear the passive voice.

With *bèi* 被:

That child was scolded by his father.
Nàge háizi bèi tā bàba mà le yídùn.
那个孩子被他爸爸骂了一顿。

Ràng 让, like *bèi* 被, is generally used with inanimate objects as the subject:

The candy was eaten by the child.
Táng ràng háizi (gěi) chī le.
糖让孩子 (给) 吃了。

NOTE: The passive voice is used much less frequently in Chinese than in English!

CHAPTER FIVE

. . . .

ADJECTIVES

(1) Adjectives: general rules

Never use *shì* 是 before adjectives!

> He is tall.
> *Tā hěn gāo*
> ✔ CC: 他很高
> ✘ BC: 他是很高!
> (noun + adjective)

BUT;

> He is a student.
> *Tā shì xuésheng.*
> 他是学生。
> (noun = noun)

We generally put *hěn* 很 (very) in front of all monosyllabic adjectives, even when we don't mean "very ___," although it isn't absolutely necessary:

We're busy.
Wǒmen hěn máng.
我们很忙。

Some Americans are fat
Yǒude Měiguó rén hěn pàng.
有的美国人很胖。

EXCEPTIONS: *è* 饿 (hungry), *kě* 渴 (thirsty), *bìng* 病 (sick), which all take *le* 了 after them rather than *hěn* 很 in front of them:

We're hungry.
Wǒmen è le.
我们饿了。

They're thirsty.
Tāmen kě le.
他们渴了。

She's ill.
✔ CC: *Tā bìng le.*
她病了。

✘ BC: *Tā hěn bìng.*
她很病。
Literally: "She is very ill/sick."

When adjectives come before a noun and are more than one syllable, including a single-syllable adjective with *hěn* 很, there is always a *de* 的 between the adjective and the noun:

very good students
hěn hǎo de xuésheng
很好的学生

pretty women
piàoliang de nǚde
漂亮的女的

handsome men
yīngjùn de nánde
英俊的男的

BUT:

good person/people
hǎo rén
好人

(2) How to translate "bad" depends on the meaning of "bad"

Use *huài* 坏, "bad," for people only, much like the word "evil" in English:

That man, bin-Laden, is really bad.
Bin-Laden nàge rén zhēn huài.
Bin-Laden 那个人真坏。

When combined with *le* 了, *huài* 坏 is used only with things, in which case it means "to go bad/spoiled/rotten"; "become wrecked/ruined"; "become useless; break down":

My car has broken down.
Wǒde chēzi huàile.
我的车子坏了。

The bananas are spoiled.
Xiāngjiāo huài le.
香蕉坏了。

When something is "bad/not good," use *bùhǎo* 不好:

That movie is bad.
Nàge diànyǐng bùhǎo.
那个电影不好。

When talking about pain or illness, use *lìhai* 厉害, "bad" in the sense of "severe/serious":

I have a bad headache.
Wǒde tóu téng de hěn lìhai.
我的头疼得很厉害。

That person has a bad cold.
Nàge rén gǎnmào de hěn lìhai.
那个人感冒得很厉害。

(3) Use *búcuò* 不错, "not bad," when you mean "quite good"

Today's weather isn't bad, is it?
Jīntiān de tiānqi búcuò, duì búduì?
今天的天气不错，对不对？

(4) Different ways to say "nice"

"Nice" is a very imprecise word in English. When referring to people, if by "nice" you mean "friendly," use *héqi* 和气, as in:

That person is very nice.
Nàge rén hěn héqi.
那个人很和气。

When by "nice" you mean "kind" or "good," use *shànliáng* 善良.

That young boy is very nice (kind). He wouldn't even
think of hurting a small bug.
*Nàge xiǎo nánhái hěn shànliáng, lián yíge xiǎo chóngzi
yě bùkěn shānghài.*
那个小男孩很善良，连一个小虫子也不肯伤害。

"Nice" when referring to the weather or something abstract, like
"nice job," is simply *hǎo* 好 (good), as in:

Today's weather is really nice.
Jīntiān de tiānqi zhēn hǎo.
今天的天气真好。

You did a nice job (You did that thing well).
Nàjian shì nǐ zuòde hěn hǎo.
那件事你做得很好。

How do you say, "Have a NICE day"? You DON'T! Of course a
person will do their best to have a nice day, but how it turns out,
the Chinese feel, is largely beyond their control.

When taking leave of someone, in place of "Have a nice day,"
simply say *Zàijiàn* 再见, "goodbye." For "Have a nice weekend,"
you can simply say "See you Monday," *Xīngqīyī jiàn* 星期一见.
These days you will hear Chinese people say something like
"Hope you have a good time" to wish people an enjoyable
weekend, as well as a good vacation, etc.:

Zhù nǐ zhōumò wánde yúkuài.
祝你周末玩得愉快。

You may even hear

Zhù nǐ yǒu yígè hǎode zhōumò.
祝你有一个好的周末
Literally: I wish you a good weekend.

But you will never hear *Zhù nǐ yǒu hǎode yìtiān* 祝你有好的一天。

(5) Different ways to say "pretty" or "beautiful," depending on the subject

Hǎokàn 好看 means "good-looking" or "attractive." It technically can only refer to people and animals, but can be used for clothing.

Piàoliang 漂亮 means "pretty" or "attractive" for women only and not men; it can also be used to describe animals as well as written characters.

Měilì 美丽 means "beautiful" and, like *piàoliang* 漂亮, can only refer to women and not men; it can, however, be used to describe scenery.

"Pretty" or "beautiful" for paintings, scenery, music, etc. is simply *měi* 美, as in:

> The scenery in Guilin is beautiful.
> *Guìlín de fēngjǐng hěn měi.*
> 桂林的风景很美。

"Pretty" when referring to music is also *hǎotīng* 好听, of course, and not *hǎokàn* 好看, since you're listening to it, not looking at it!

(6) Comparisons: A *bǐ* 比 B

Positive comparisons: How to say something or someone is more ___ than something or someone else, as in smaller, cheaper, faster, etc.:

> A "compared to" B is ___
> A *bǐ* 比 B [adjective] *or* [verb clause]

Japan is smaller than China.
Rìběn bǐ Zhōngguó xiǎo.
日本比中国小。
Literally: Japan compared to China is small.

Planes are faster than trains, but are more expensive than trains.
Fēijī bǐ huǒchē kuài, kěshi bǐ huǒchē guì.
飞机比火车快，可是比火车贵。
Literally: Planes compared to trains are fast, but compared to trains are expensive.

It is incorrect to substitute *bǐjiào* 比较 for *bǐ* 比 in these cases; *bǐjiào* 比较 means "relatively," not "compared to . . . ":

That chair is relatively expensive. How about buying this chair?
Nèi bǎ yǐzi bǐjiào guì, nǐ mǎi zhèi bǎ yǐzi ba.
那把椅子比较贵，你买这把椅子吧。

much more or much less . . .
A 比 B + adjective + 多了/得多

To indicate degree of comparison, i.e. "much more . . . " or "a little more . . . ," add *de duō* 得多 or *duō le* 多了 after the adjective or verb clause for "much more. . . ."

NOTE: *hěn* 很 CANNOT be used in comparisons!

Cars are much faster than bicycles.
✔ CC: *Qìchē bǐ zìxíngchē kuài de duō* (or *kuài duō le).*
汽车比自行车快得多 (快多了)。

✘ BC: *Qìchē bǐ zìxíngchē hěn kuài.*
汽车比自行车很快。

Add *yìdiǎn(r)* 一点／一点儿 after the adjective or verb clause to express "a little more . . .":

> a little more . . . ; a little less . . .
> A *bǐ* 比 B + adjective + *yidian(r)*

> The U.S. is a little bigger than China.
> *Měiguó bǐ Zhōngguó dà yìdiǎn(r).*
> 美国比中国大一点 (儿) 。

Note: *Bǐ* 比 cannot be used in sentences with *yíyàng* 一样 (same) or with *bùyíyàng* 不一样 (not the same). Instead, use *gēn* 跟 or *hé* 和. After all, in English we don't say, "Some Japanese customs compared to some Chinese customs are/aren't the same," but rather, "Some Japanese customs AND some Chinese customs are/aren't the same":

> Some Japanese customs are the same as (some) Chinese customs.
> *Yǒude Rìběn fēngsú xíguàn gēn Zhōngguó de fēngsú xíguàn yíyàng.*
> 有的日本风俗习惯跟中国的风俗习惯一样。
> Literally: Some Japanese customs and (some) Chinese customs are the same.

> Some Japanese customs aren't the same as (some) Chinese customs.
> *Yǒude Rìběn fēngsú xíguàn gēn Zhōngguó de fēngsú xíguàn bù yíyàng.*
> 有的日本风俗习惯跟中国的风俗习惯不一样。
> Literally: Some Japanese customs and (some) Chinese customs aren't the same.

(7) Negative comparisons: A is not as [adjective] as B

To express "A doesn't have B's __" (can be a positive or negative attribute), use A *méiyǒu* 没有 B (*nàme* 那么) ___:

I'm not as good-looking as you are.
Wǒ méiyǒu nǐ (nàme) hǎokàn.
我没有你 (那么) 好看。

You're not as fat as I am.
Nǐ méiyǒu wǒ (nàme) pàng.
你没有我 (那么) 胖。

To express "A can't compare to B's ____" (always refers to a positive attribute and is a bit more formal), use A *bùrú* 不如 B (*nàme* 那么) ____ :

I'm not as smart as you.
Wǒ bùrú nǐ cōngmíng.
我不如你聪明。

CHAPTER SIX

· ·

VARIOUS USES OF THE PARTICLE *LE* 了

(1) *Le* 了 is used after action verbs in the past tense

Only with a simple verb-object compound, such as *kànshū* 看书 or *chīfàn* 吃饭, can you put a *le* 了 either after the verb or after the direct object:

> She read a book.
> *Tā kàn le shū.*   OR   *Tā kánshū le.*
> 她看了书。OR   她看书了。

> She ate (a meal).
> *Tā chīle fàn.*   OR   *Tā chīfàn le.*
> 她吃了饭。OR   她吃饭了。

BUT, if you put the *le* 了 right after the verb and before the direct object, it implies someone has just done something in the immediate past ("has/have just read a book"; "has/have just eaten a meal"). If you put the *le* 了 after the direct object, it implies someone did something in the not so immediate past ("read a book or did read a book"; "ate a meal or did eat a meal").

There are two simple verb-object compounds, however, where the *le* 了 tends to always come after the direct object, namely *shuìjiào* 睡觉 and *sànbù* 散步. These are verbs that tend to only take one particular direct object. You can eat (吃) many different things and you can read/look at (看) various things, but sleep 睡 can only take 觉 as a direct object, for example:

> She fell asleep./She slept.
> *Tā shuìjiào le.*
> 她睡觉了。

If the direct object is not a simple generic one, like *fàn* 饭 or *shū* 书, but more specific and therefore longer, such as *Zhōngguó fàn* 中国饭 or *hěn duō Zhōngwén shū* 很多中文书, then *le* 了 always comes right after the verb and before the direct object, regardless of when in the past it occurred.

> I ate Chinese food.
> *Wǒ chī le Zhōngguó fàn.*
> 我吃了中国饭。

> My friend read a lot of Chinese books.
> *Wǒde péngyou kàn le hěn duō Zhōngwén shū.*
> 我的朋友看了很多中文书。

However, if there is a sequence of action verbs, where you want to say that after doing one thing, someone did something else, then the *le* 了 directly follows the first action verb but for the final verb in the sequence the *le* 了 comes after the direct object and at the end of the sentence.

> After eating (having eaten) dinner, I fell asleep.
> *Wǒ chīle wǎnfàn jiù shuìjiào le.*
> 我吃了晚饭就睡觉了。

If it's a sequence of events in the present or future tense, where you're saying that having done one thing someone does or will do another, then the *le* 了 comes after the first verb in the sequence and there is no *le* 了 at the end of the sentence.

> After eating (having eaten dinner, I study.
> *Wǒ chīle wǎnfàn jiù niànshū.*
> 我吃了晚饭就念书。

> After eating (having eaten) dinner, I'll go see a movie.
> *Wǒ chīle wǎnfàn jiù huì qù kàn diànyǐng.*
> 我吃了晚饭就会去看电影。

If you list a number of things you did, then the *le* 了 comes after the action verb and before the direct object for every verb except the last one, for which the *le* 了 comes at the end, after the direct object.

> Yesterday I ate dinner, studied, watched TV, and then went to sleep.
> *Wǒ zuótiān chīle wǎnfàn, niànle shū, kànle diànshì jiù shuìjiào le.*
> 我昨天吃了晚饭，念了书，看了电视就睡觉了。

WHEN *le* 了 is placed BOTH after the verb AND at the end of the sentence, then the implication is that the action occurred in the past and is still going on.

> He has read two books (and is still continuing to read).
> *Tā kàn le liǎngběn shū le.*
> 他看了两本书了。

> I have studied Chinese for two years (and am still studying it).
> *Wǒ xuéle liángnián de Zhōngwén le.*
> 我学了两年的中文了。

NOTE the difference between "did" something and "have done" something, *le* 了 vs. *guò* 过:

Last year she went to China.
Tā qùnián qùle Zhōngguó.
她去年去了中国。

BUT:

She's been to China, so she has eaten real Chinese food.
Tā qùguò Zhōngguó , suǒyǐ tā chīguò zhēnzhèngde Zhōngguó cài.
她去过中国，所以她吃过真正的中国菜。

(2) *Le* 了 is used after adjectives to express "change of status," i.e. "became . . . "

She's gotten fat.
Tā pàng le.
她胖了。

She's hungry (now).
Tā è le.
她饿了。

(3) *Le* 了 is used after verbs to express "imminent action," i.e., something just about to happen

We're leaving (now).
Wǒmen zǒu le.
我们走了。

We're about to eat.
Wǒmen yào chīfàn le!
我们要吃饭了！

(4) *Le* 了 is used with verbs or adjectives in the negative to express "not any more"

He doesn't drink alcohol any more.
Tā bù hē jiǔ le.
他不喝酒了。

She isn't fat any more.
Tā búpàng le.
她不胖了。

CHAPTER SEVEN

. . . .

VARIOUS USES OF THE PARTICLE *DE*:
DE 的 VS. *DE* 得 VS. *DE* 地

The character you choose for the particle *de* in Chinese depends on the usage.

(1) The uses of *de* 的

To separate two nouns, including to indicate possession, use 的:

> my book
> *wǒ de shū*
> 我的书

> economic problems
> *jīngjì de wèntí*
> 经济的问题

To separate adjectives from nouns when the adjective is put before the noun, use 的:

a very large family (or very large families)
✔ *CC: hěn dà de jiātíng*
很大的家庭

✘ *BC:* 很大的家!
a very large home (or very large homes)

pretty girls
piàoliang de gūniáng
漂亮的姑娘

To put a descriptive phrase in front of a noun in "that" and "who" clauses (i.e. "the thing that . . . " or "the person who . . . "), use *de* 的:

the book that I bought yesterday
Wǒ zuótiān mǎide shū
我昨天买的书

the people who bought that book
Mǎi nèiběn shū de rén
买那本书的人

(2) The uses of *de* 得

Use *de* 得 after verbs to indicate HOW something is done (well or poorly, quickly or slowly, etc.):

My older brother drives too fast!
Wǒ gēge kāichē kāide tài kuài.
我哥哥开车开得太快。

You speak English very well.
Nǐ shuō Yīngyǔ shuōde hěn hǎo.
你说英语说得很好。

Use *de* 得 after adjectives to mean "so ... that ...":

> I was so happy that I started to jump (for joy).
> *Wǒ gāoxìng de tiàoqǐlái le.*
> 我高兴得跳起来了。

> My older sister was so sad she started to cry.
> *Wǒ jiějie nánguò de kūqǐlái le.*
> 我姐姐难过得哭起来了。

(3) The uses of *de* 地

Use *de* 地 between an adjective and a verb, to say "quickly," "slowly," "badly," etc.:

> They are speaking (chatting) happily.
> *Tāmen gāoxìng de liáotiān (tántan).*
> 他们高兴地聊天 (谈谈) 。

> You ought to eat slowly.
> *Nǐ yīnggāi mànman de chīfàn.*
> 你应该慢慢地吃饭。

CHAPTER EIGHT

· ·

CONJUNCTIONS: AND, OR

(1) Different ways to say "and" depend on usage

Used to connect nouns, "and" can be *hé* 和 or gēn 跟:

> You and I are good friends.
> *Nǐ hé wǒ shì hǎo péngyou.*
> 你和我是好朋友。

> My friend and I went to China.
> *Wǒde péngyou gēn wǒ dào Zhōngguó qùle.*
> 我的朋友跟我到中国去了。

HOWEVER, with a string of nouns, instead of a word for "and," simply place a special Chinese comma between the nouns:

> Tofu, *jiaozi*, and spring rolls are all Chinese food.
> *Dòufu, jiǎozi, chūnjuǎn dōu shì Zhōngguó cài.*
> 豆腐、饺子、春卷都是中国菜。

Used to connect verbs or adjectives, "and" is *yě* 也:

Today I went to class and studied.
Wǒ jīntiān shàng le kè yě niàn le shū.
我今天上了课也念了书。

She's tall and slender.
Tā hěn gāo yě hěn miáotiao.
她很高也很苗条。

(2) How to say "or" in Chinese

To use "or" in a statement: choose between the formal, *huòshi*
或是, and the informal *huòzhě* 或者:

Every morning I drink tea or coffee
Wǒ měitiān zǎoshàng hē chá huòshì (huòzhě) hē kāfēi.
我每天早上喝茶或是 (或者) 喝咖啡。

To use "either . . . or . . . ," choose between the more emphatic
and the less formal:

either . . . or . . . (more emphatic)
huòshi . . . huòshi . . .
或是 . . . 或是 . . .

OR:

either . . . or . . . (less formal)
huòzhě . . . huòzhě . . .
或者 . . . 或者 . . .

Every morning I either drink tea or coffee.
Wǒ měitiān zǎoshàng huòshì (huòzhe) hē chá huòshì
(huòzhě) hē kāfēi.
我每天早上或是 (或者) 喝茶或是 (或者) 喝咖啡。

To use "or" in a question, use *háishì* 还是:

In the morning do you drink tea or (do you drink) coffee?
Nǐ zǎoshàng hē chá háishì (hē) kāfēi?
你早上喝茶还是 (喝) 咖啡?

CHAPTER NINE

· ·

SUBORDINATE CLAUSES

(1) Connecting sentences with "who"/"that"

There are no connecting words for "who" or "that" in Chinese, so whatever clause modifies a noun comes before it, not afterward. There is no preceding "who" or "that" as in English:

> English: The house that Jack built is big.
> Chinese: The Jack-built house is big.
> *Jack gàide fángzi hěn dà.*
> Jack盖的房子很大。

> English: The meal that my Chinese friend cooked was delicious.
> Chinese: My Chinese friend('s) cooked meal was delicious.
> *Wǒde Zhōngguó péngyou zuòde fàn hěn hǎochī.*
> 我的中国朋友做的饭很好吃。

> English: Students who study Chinese are the smartest students.
> Chinese: Studying Chinese students are the smartest students.
> *Xué Zhōngwén de xuésheng shì zuì cōngmíngde xuésheng.*
> 学中文的学生是最聪明的学生。

(2) In Chinese, "if . . . then . . ." is expressed in three levels of formality

Most formal: *rúguǒ . . . jiù . . .* 如果 . . . 就 . . .
Less formal: *yàoshi . . . jiù . . .* 要是 . . . 就 . . .
Least formal: *. . . de huà, jiù . . . . . .* 的话，就 . . .

The IF clause ALWAYS comes first, and the second clause needs a *jiù* 就. Moreover, the subject in the second clause must come BEFORE *jiù* 就:

English: If you go, then I'll go.
Chinese: If you go, I'll (then) go.
Rúguǒ nǐ qù, wǒ jiù qù.
如果你去，我就去。

OR:

Yàoshi nǐ qù, wǒ jiù qù.
要是你去，我就去。

OR:

Nǐ qù de huà, wǒ jiù qù.
你去的话，我就去。

For emphasis, you can combine *rúguǒ . . . jiù . . .* 如果 . . . 就 . . . with *. . . de huà* 的话:

If you (should) go, then I'll go.
Rúguǒ nǐ qù de huà, wǒ jiù qù.
如果你去的话，我就去。

OR:

Yàoshi nǐ qù de huà, wǒ jiù qù.
要是你去的话，我就去。

BUT, when the subject is the same in both clauses, there is no need to repeat the subject:

If you're sick, (then) don't go.
Yàoshi (rúguǒ) nǐ bìngle, jiù búyòng qù.
要是 (如果) 你病了，就不用去。

(3) "As soon as . . . (then) . . ." = *yī . . . jiù . . .* 一 . . . 就 . . .

Yī 一 plus a verb, meaning "as soon as," must always be followed by *jiù* 就:

As soon as he saw her, he (then) fell in love with her.
Tā yí kànjian tā, jiù àishang tā le.
他一看见她就爱上她了。

Note: *jiù* 就 in the second clause can NEVER be put in FRONT of a noun:

As soon as I return home, (then) I do my homework.
✔ CC: *Yì huíjiā, wǒ jiù zuò gōngkè.*
一回家，我就做功课。

✘ BC: *Yì huíjiā, jiù wǒ zuò gōngkè.*
一回家，就我做功课。

(4) "Even . . . (also) . . . " = *lián . . . , yě/dōu . . .* 连 . . . , 也/都 . . .

The *lián* 连 (even) clause always comes first in Chinese and must be followed by *yě* 也 (also):

Even my best friend doesn't know.
Lián wǒ zuì hǎo de péngyou yě (dōu) bù zhīdao.
连我最好的朋友也 (都) 不知道。

More formally, "even . . . (also) . . ." = *shènzhì . . . yě/dōu . . .*
甚至 . . . 也/都 . . . :

Even Chinese people can't write every Chinese character.
Shènzhì Zhōngguó rén yě (dōu) búhuì xiě suǒyǒude Hànzì.
甚至中国人也 (都) 不会写所有的汉字。

(5) "Because . . . , so . . ." = *yīnwei . . . , suǒyǐ . . .*
因为. . . , 所以 . . .

In any sentence that begins with *yīnwei* 因为, the second clause must start with *suǒyǐ* 所以, even though in English we don't generally put "so" or "therefore" in the second clause):

Because I'm tired, (so) I'm going to bed.
Yīnwei wǒ lèile, suǒyǐ wǒ yào shàngchuáng.
因为我累了，所以我要上床。

(6) "It doesn't matter . . ." = *wúlùn . . . dōu . . .*
无论 . . . 都 . . .

It doesn't matter who comes, he (still) won't see them.
Wúlùn shéi lái, tā dōu bújiàn.
无论谁来，他都不见。

It doesn't matter what it is, I (still) don't want to eat it.
Wúlùn shì shénme, wǒ dōu bùxiǎng chī.
无论是什么，我都不想吃。

To say "it doesn't matter whether . . . " when there are two alternatives, use *wúlùn* (two alternatives) *dōu* . . . :

> It doesn't matter whether you want to go or not, you (still) must go.
> *Wúlùn nǐ xiǎng qù bùxiǎng qù, nǐ dōu děi qù.*
> 无论你想去不想去，你都得去。

(7) "Besides . . . " = *chúle . . . yǐwài* 除了 . . . 以外

"Besides" in the sense of "with the exception of . . . ":

> *Chúle . . . yǐwài, dōu . . .*
> 除了 . . . 以外，都 . . .

> Besides Mr. Li, everyone can speak English.
> *Chúle Lǐ Xiānsheng yǐwài, dàjiā dōu huì shuō Yīngyǔ.*
> 除了李先生以外，大家都会说英语。

"Besides" in the sense of "in addition to . . . ":

> *Chúle . . . yǐwài, hái . . .*
> 除了 . . . 以外，还 . . .

> Besides Chinese, I can also speak Japanese.
> *Chúle Hànyǔ yǐwài, wǒ hái huì shuō Rìyǔ.*
> 除了汉语以外，我还会说日语。

CHAPTER TEN

. . . .

HOW TO EXPRESS THE VERB "CAN" IN CHINESE

(A HUGE CAN OF WORMS!)

How to translate "can" depends on its meaning.

To express "can"/"know how to," use *huì* 会:

I can/know how to speak Chinese.
Wǒ huì shuō Hànyǔ.
我会说汉语。

I can/know how to play the piano.
Wǒ huì tán gāngqín.
我会弹钢琴。

To express "can"/"able to" (physically), use *néng* 能:

I'm very strong and can do mountain climbing.
Wǒ hěn zhuàng, wǒ néng páshān.
我很壮，我能爬山。

I have a heart condition and can't run.
Wǒ yǒu xīnzàngbìng, bùnéng pǎo.
我有心脏病，不能跑。

THEREFORE:

My little brother is eight months old. He can't speak.
Wǒ xiǎo dìdi bāge yuè, búhuì shuōhuà.
我小弟弟八个月，不会说话。

BUT:

My little sister is a deaf mute. She can't speak.
Wǒ mèimei shì lóngyǎ rén, tā bù néng shuōhuà.
我妹妹是聋哑人，她不能说话。

To express "can"/"may"/"are permitted to," use *kěyǐ* 可以:

We can/may/are permitted to speak Chinese in Chinese
class; we may not speak English.
Zài shàng Hànyǔ kè shí, wǒmen kěyǐ shuō Hànyǔ,
bùkěyǐ shuō Yīngyǔ.
在上汉语课时，我们可以说汉语，不可以说英语。

Use resultative endings to express "can" and "can't." There
are many verbs in Chinese that do not use *huì* 会 or *néng* 能 to
express the ability to do something. Rather, according to what
type of verb they are, many of them take a special resultative
ending to express the idea of "can"/"able to." Below is a list of
the most commonly used of these types of verbs:

Verbs of Senses: *-jiàn* 见 or *-dào* 到
_____

can see
kàndejiàn or *kàndedào*
看得见 or 看得到

can't see
kànbujiàn or *kànbudào*
看不见 or 看不到

can hear
tīngdejiàn or *tīngdedào*
听得见 or 听得到

can't hear
tīngbujiàn or *tīngbudào*
听不见 or 听不到

can smell
wéndejiàn or *wéndedào*
闻得见 or 闻得到

can't smell
wénbujiàn or *wénbudào*
闻不见 or 闻不到

BUT:

can taste
✔ *CC: chángdedào*
尝得到

✖ *BC: chángdejiàn*
尝得见

can't taste
chángbudào
尝不到

AND:

can touch/feel
✔ *CC: mōdedào*
摸得到

✖ *BC: mōdejiàn*
摸得见

can't touch/feel
mōbudào
摸不到

To express "can or can't understand by ___ing," use -*dǒng* -懂:

can understand (by reading)
kàndedǒng
看得懂

can't understand
kànbudǒng
看不懂

can understand (by listening)
tīngdedǒng
听得懂

can't understand
tīngbudǒng
听不懂

To express "___ clearly," use -*qīngchu* 清楚:

can see clearly
kàndeqīngchu
看得清楚

can't see clearly
kànbuqīngchu
看不清楚

can hear clearly
tīngdeqīngchu
听得清楚

can't hear clearly
tīngbuqīngchu
听不清楚

To express successful completion of an action, use -*zháo* 着 or
-*dào* 到:

can find
zhǎodezháo or *zhǎodedào*
找得着 or 找得到

can't find
zhǎobuzháo or *zhǎobudào*
找不着 or 找不到

can buy
mǎidezháo or *mǎidedào*
买得着 or 买得到

can't buy (because not available)
mǎibuzháo or *mǎibudào*
买不着 or 买不到

To express the ability to do something physical, use -*liǎo* 了:

can carry
nádeliǎo
拿得了

can't carry
nábuliǎo
拿不了

can say (physically able to say)
shuōdeliǎo
说得了

can't say
shuōbuliǎo
说不了

To express "can afford to," use -*qǐ* 起:

can afford to buy
mǎideqǐ
买得起

can't afford to buy
mǎibuqǐ
买不起

can afford to pay
fùdeqǐ
付得起

can't afford to pay
fùbuqǐ
付不起

can afford to face someone (figuratively)
duìdeqǐ
对得起

can't afford to face someone (because you've done something shameful)
duìbuqǐ
对不起

To express "can ___ up," use -*qǐlái* 起来:

can pick up
nádeqǐlái
拿得起来

can't pick up
nábuqǐlái
拿不起来

can pull up
lādeqǐlái
拉得起来

can't pull up
lābuqǐlái
拉不起来

can stand up
zhàndeqǐlái
站得起来

can't stand up
zhànbuqǐlái
站不起来

To express "can __ out," use -*chūlái* 出来:

can take out
nádechūlái
拿得出来

can't take out
nábuchūlái
拿不出来

can speak out
shuōdechūlái
说得出来

can't speak out
shuōbuchūlái
说不出来

To express "keep/remain ___ in," use -*zhù* 住:

> can hold on to
> *nádezhù*
> 拿得住

> can't hold on to
> *nábuzhù*
> 拿不住

> can keep standing
> *zhàndezhù*
> 站得住

> can't keep standing; can't stay in business
> *zhànbuzhù*
> 站不住

To express "can finish doing something," use -*wán* 完:

> can finish doing something
> *zuòdewán*
> 做得完

> can finish speaking/saying something
> *shuōdewán*
> 说得完

To negate all these, replace *de* 得 with *bu* 不, as in previous examples.

To express "to ___ up(stairs)," use *shànglái* 上来 or *shàngqu* 上去:

> to walk up(stairs) [to where the speaker currently is]
> *zǒushàng(lóu)lái*
> 走上 (楼) 来

to walk up(stairs) [away from where the speaker is]
zǒushàng(lóu)qù
走上 (楼) 去

to run up(stairs) [to where the speaker is]
pǎoshàng(lóu)lái
跑上 (楼) 来

to run up(stairs) [away from where the speaker is]
pǎoshàng (lóu) qù
跑上 (楼) 去

To express "to ___ down(stairs)," use *xiàlái* 下来 or *xiàqu* 下去:

to walk down(stairs) [to where the speaker is]
zǒuxià (lóu) lái
走下 (楼) 来

to walk down(stairs) [away from the speaker]
zǒuxià (lóu) qù
走下 (楼) 去

CHAPTER ELEVEN

∙ ∙

WORD-CHOICE ISSUES WITH CERTAIN
IMPORTANT VERBS

(1) "To be a . . . (profession, friend, etc.)": differences between *shì* 是, *dāng* 当, and *zuò* 做

Shì 是 is simply the verb "to be":

> She is a doctor.
> *Tā shì yīsheng.*
> 她是医生。

> They are my friends.
> *Tāmen shì wǒde péngyou.*
> 他们是我的朋友

Dāng 当 is "to be" in the sense of "to serve as," and is always followed by a certain profession or official position:

> She is a doctor at that hospital.
> *Tā zài nàge yīyuàn dāng yīsheng.*
> 她在那个医院当医生。

He is (serving as) the head of the English Department:
Ta dāng Yīngyǔxì de xìzhǔrèn.
他当英语系的系主任。

Zuò 做 as "to be" is less formal than *dāng* 当 and is broader in meaning. It can refer to being something other than the holder of a profession or office, such as "to be a parent" or "to be a brother/sister":

Anyone who is an older brother or sister ought to take of their younger siblings.
Zuò gēge jiějie de yīnggāi zhàogu dìdi mèimei.
做哥哥姐姐的应该照顾弟弟妹妹。

(2) "To know": *zhīdao* 知道 vs. *rènshi* 认识 vs. *huì* 会

To say "to know a fact" or "to know of someone," use *zhīdao* 知道:

I know (that) she's Chinese.
Wǒ zhīdao tā shì Zhōngguó rén.
我知道她是中国人。

I know of (have heard of) her.
Wǒ zhīdao tā.
我知道她。

When you mean "to know a person, place, or Chinese character" or "to meet someone," use *rènshi* 认识:

I know that professor.
Wǒ rènshi nèige jiàoshòu.
我认识那个教授。

I know that character.
Wǒ rènshi nàge zì.
✔ *CC:* 我认识那个字。

✘ *BC:* 我知道那个字。

SO:

I know of that professor, but I don't know him personally.
Wǒ zhīdao nèige jiàoshou, dànshi wǒ búrènshi tā.
我知道那个教授，但是我不认识他。

I know that painting.
✔ *CC: Wǒ zhīdao nàzhāng huà.*
我知道那张画。

✘ *BC: Wǒ rènshi nàzhāng huà.*
我认识那张画。

To say "know how to do something," use *huì* 会:

My wife really knows how to cook.
Wǒ tàitai zhēn huì zuòfàn.
我太太真会做饭。

I know how to write some Chinese characters.
Wǒ huì xiě yīxie Hànzì.
我会写一些汉字。

(3) The difference between "to like" *xǐhuān* 喜欢 and "would like to" *xiǎng* 想

Do you like to watch movies?
Nǐ xǐhuān kàn diànyǐng ma?
你喜欢看电影吗？

Would you like to watch a movie?
Nǐ xiǎng kàn diànyǐng ma?
你想看电影吗？

THEREFORE:

I would like to look at that thing. [said to salesperson]
✔ CC: *Wǒ xiǎng kànkan nàge dōngxi.*
我想看看那个东西。

✘ BC: *Wǒ xǐhuān kàn nàge dōngxi.*
我喜欢看那个东西。
Literally: I like to look at that thing . . . and nothing else!

You would never say to a salesperson:

I like to buy this.
✘ BC: *Wǒ xǐhuān mǎi zhèige*
我喜欢买这个。

Instead, you would say:

I would like to buy this.
✔ CC: *Wǒ xiǎng mǎi zhèige*
我想买这个 。

(4) The difference between "to think that . . . ," *xiǎng* 想, and "to feel . . . ," *juéde* 觉得

Xiǎng 想 and *juéde* 觉得 can be used interchangeably IF by "feel" you mean "feel that . . . ":

Do you think that movie is good?
Nǐ xiǎng nàge diànyǐng hǎo ma?
你想那个电影好吗？

Do you feel that that movie is good?
Nǐ juéde nàge diànyǐng hǎo ma?
你觉得那个电影好吗？

BUT:

What do you feel like doing?
Nǐ xiǎng zuò shénme?
你想做什么？

How do you feel? Do you feel poorly?
Nǐ juéde zěnme yàng? Nǐ juéde bùshūfu ma?
你觉得怎么样？你觉得不舒服吗？

I feel like taking a walk.
✔ *CC: Wǒ xiǎng sànbù.*
我想散步。

✘ *BC: Wǒ juéde sànbù.*
我觉得散步。

(5) "To want/would like (to do something)": *xiǎng* 想 vs. *yào* 要 vs. *xiǎngyào* 想要

When you say you want something, whether a concrete object like a car or something abstract like friendship, you cannot use *xiǎng* 想. When the word "want" is followed by a noun, you must use either *yào* 要 or *xiǎngyào* 想要.

I'd like a bottle of beer.
✔ *CC: Wǒ yào yìpíng píjiǔ.*
我要一瓶啤酒。

OR:

✔ *CC: Wǒ xiǎngyào yìpíng píjiǔ.*
我想要一瓶啤酒。

✘ *BC: Wǒ xiǎng yìpíng píjiǔ.*
我想一瓶啤酒。
I am thinking of a bottle of beer" rather than thinking of anything else!

She wants a handsome boyfriend.
✔ *CC: Tā yào yíge yīngjùnde nánpéngyou.*
她要一个英俊的男朋友。

OR:

✔ *CC: Tā xiǎngyào yíge yīngjùnde nánpéngyou.*
她想要一个英俊的男朋友。

✘ *BC: Tā xiǎng yíge yīngjùnde nánpéngyou.*
她想一个英俊的男朋友。
She is thinking of a handsome boyfriend.

BUT, when you want or would like to do something, i.e., when the word "want" is followed by a verb, you may use *xiǎng* 想 as a softer, more polite way to say *yào* 要:

I'd like to drink a bottle of beer.
Wǒ xiǎng hē yìpíng píjiǔ.
我想喝一瓶啤酒。

She'd like to find a handsome boyfriend.
Tā xiǎng zhǎo yíge yīngjùnde nánpéngyou.
她想找一个英俊的男朋友。

ALSO, be aware that when you use *yào* 要 to tell someone you want something, it is tantamount to a direct command.

You may say to a waiter:

I want (a) broccoli beef.
Wǒ yào yíge jièlán niúròu.
我要一个芥兰牛肉。

BUT it would soften your wishes and be more polite to say:

I would like (a) broccoli beef.
Wǒ xiǎngyào yíge jièlán niúròu.
我想要一个芥兰牛肉。

(6) Rude vs. refined: *yào* 要 vs. *xiǎngyào* 想要

RUDE:

What do you want to drink?
Nǐ yào hē shénme?
你要喝什么？

I want (to drink) some tea.
Wǒ yào hē chá.
我要喝茶。

REFINED:

What would you like to drink?
Nǐ xiǎng hē shénme?
你想喝什么？

I'd like some tea, please.
✔ *CC: Wǒ xiǎng hē (yì) diǎn chá.*
我想喝点茶。

✘ *BC:* 我想茶。

NOTE: This is incorrect because *xiǎng* 想 cannot be directly followed by a noun.

✖ *BC:* 我想一些茶，请。

NOTE: This is wrong on THREE counts, because *xiǎng* 想 cannot be directly followed by a noun when it means "would like to"; because *yīxiē* 一些 means "some" of a group of things; and finally because *qǐng* 请 is never used at the end of a sentence, but always before a verb. Worst of all, you will have violated the #1 cardinal rule of translation, which is to NEVER, EVER translate literally!

(7) "I don't think that . . . ": don't even THINK about using *bùxiǎng* 不想!

In English, we say: "I don't think (that) he's coming tonight" or "I don't think (that) what he said is right." But in Chinese, you cannot say "I don't think that . . . ," because, to the Chinese way of thinking, how can you have an opinion if you don't think?!

I don't think (that) he's coming tonight.
✔ *CC: Wǒ xiǎng tā jīntiān wǎnshang búhuì lái.*
我想他今天晚上不会来。

✖ *BC: Wǒ bùxiǎng tā jīntiān wǎnshang huì lái.*
我不想他今天晚上会来。

I don't think (that) what he said is right.
✔ *CC: Wǒ xiǎng tā shuōde búduì.*
我想他说得不对。

✖ *BC: Wǒ bùxiǎng tā shuōde duì.*
我不想他说得对。

BUT, we do use *bùxiǎng* 不想 WHEN we mean that we don't feel like doing something or don't intend to do something.

I don't feel like going/don't intend to go.
Wǒ bùxiǎng qù.
我不想去。

I don't feel like eating it.
Wǒ bùxiǎng chī
我不想吃。

(8) "To want someone to be . . .": *xiǎngyào* 想要 vs. *xīwang* 希望 vs. *bìxū* 必须

When saying you want someone to be a certain way, only if that person is someone over whom you have control, generally your children, you can use *xiǎngyào* 想要 to mean "want":

> I want my son to be (become) an engineer.
> ✔ *CC: Wǒ xiǎngyào wǒde érzi chéngwéi yíge gōngchéngshī.*
> 我想要我的儿子成为一个工程师。

> ✘ *BC: Wǒ xiǎng wǒde érzi chéngwéi yíge gōngchéngshī.*
> 我想我的儿子成为一个工程师。
> Literally: I am thinking my son become an engineer. [It's that nonsensical in Chinese!]

BUT if you want any adult, including a spouse or boyfriend/girlfriend, to be a certain way, you can only say that you "hope," *xīwang* 希望, they will be that way:

> I want my (ideal) boyfriend to be a good Christian.
> ✔ *CC: Wǒ xīwàng wǒde nánpéngyou shì yíge hǎo Jīdūtú.*
> 我希望我的男朋友是一个好基督徒。

> ✘ *BC: Wǒ xiǎngyào wǒde nánpéngyou shì yíge hǎo Jīdūtú.*
> 我想要我的男朋友是一个好基督徒。

To change your wish for how you'd like someone to be into a firm requirement, then use *bìxū* 必须 (must):

> My (ideal) boyfriend must be a good Christian.
> *Wǒde nánpéngyou bìxū shì yíge hǎo Jīdūtú.*
> 我的男朋友必须是一个好基督徒。

(9) How to translate "to ask" depends on the meaning of "ask": *wèn* 问 vs. *qǐng* 请 vs. *jiào* 叫

To "ask" (a question) or "inquire," use *wèn* 问 :

> I asked him whether you were coming or not.
> ✔ *CC: Wǒ wèn tā nǐ lái bùlái.*
> 我问他你来不来。

> ✘ *BC: Wǒ wènle tā nǐ lái bùlái.*
> 我问了他你来不来。

To "ask/invite" (someone to do something), use *qǐng* 请 :

> I asked/invited her to eat dinner with me.
> *Wǒ qǐng tā gēn wǒ chī wǎnfàn. .*
> 我请她跟我吃晚饭。

To "ask/tell" (somebody to do something), use *jiào* 叫:

> I asked my little sister to phone me:
> *Wǒ jiào wǒ mèimei gěi wǒ dǎ diànhua.*
> 我叫我妹妹给我打电话。

NOTE: *jiào* 叫 is only used in regard to people who are younger or in a lower social position than the person asking or telling them to do something. It therefore cannot be used to ask or tell a parent, teacher, boss, or official to do something. In those cases, *qǐng* 请 would be used.

> I asked my mother to call (phone) me.
> ✔ *CC: Wǒ qǐng wǒ māma gěi wǒ dǎ diànhuà.*
> 我请我妈妈给我打电话。

> ✘ *BC: Wǒ jiào wǒ māma gěi wǒ dǎ diànhuà.*
> 我叫我妈妈给我打电话。

(10) How to translate "to tell" depends on the meaning of "tell": *shuō* 说 vs. *jiǎng* 讲 vs. *jiào* 叫 vs. *gàosu* 告诉 vs. *ràng* 让

To "tell," in the sense of to "say" something to someone, use *shuō* 说:

> She told me she loved me.
> *Tā duì wǒ shuō tā ài wǒ.*
> 她对我说她爱我。

To "tell" (a story), use *jiǎng* 讲:

> She told a strange story.
> *Tā jiǎng le yíge hěn qíguàide gùshi.*
> 她讲了一个很奇怪的故事。

To "tell" (someone to do something), use *jiào* 叫:

> She told me to call her.
> *Tā jiào wǒ gěi tā dǎ diànhuà.*
> 她叫我给她打电话。

To "tell"/"inform" (someone about something), use *gàosu* 告诉:

> My Mom told me my dog died:
> *Wǒ māma gàosu wǒ wǒde gǒu sǐle.*
> 我妈妈告诉我我的狗死了。

To "tell"/"have"/"make" (someone do something), use *ràng* 让:

> My Mom told me/made me/had me study.
> *Wǒ māma ràng wǒ niànshū.*
> 我妈妈让我念书。

(11) "To look like" and "to seem like": *xiàng* 像 and *hǎoxiàng* 好像

Use *xiàng* 像 to say "to look like . . ." in the sense of "to resemble . . ."

> She looks like her mother.
> ✔ CC: *Tā xiàng tā mǔqin.*
> 她像她母亲。
>
> ✘ BC: *Tā hǎoxiàng tā mǔqin.*
> 她好像她母亲。

Use *hǎoxiàng* 好像 to say "to look like . . ." in the sense of "to seem like"; "to appear that . . .":

> It looks like/seems like it's going to rain.
> *Hǎoxiàng huì xiàyǔ.*
> 好像会下雨。

(12) "Receive": know the difference between the two characters pronounced *shou* in Chinese (*shōu* 收, *shòu* 受), both of which mean "receive"

Shōudào 收到 means to receive something concrete:

> to receive a letter
> *shōudào yìfēng xìn*
> 收到一封信

> to receive a present
> *shōudào yífèn lǐwù*
> 收到一份礼物

Shòudào 受到 means to "receive" something abstract, such as an influence, protection, etc. It is always used in passive voice:

> to receive protection (be protected)
> *shòudào bǎohù*
> 受到保护

> to receive influence (be influenced)
> *shòudào yǐngxiǎng*
> 受到影响

(13) "Afraid": know the difference between "to be afraid," *hàipà* 害怕, "to be afraid of . . . ," *pà* 怕, and "to be afraid that . . . ," *kǒngpà* 恐怕

> Don't be afraid!
> *Bié hàipa!*
> 别害怕！

> I'm afraid of snakes.
> *Wǒ pà shé.*
> 我怕蛇。

> I'm afraid that she's afraid of snakes.
> *Kǒngpà tā pà shé.*
> 恐怕她怕蛇。

(14) "Worry": the subtle differences between *dānxīn* 担心, *cāoxīn* 操心, *fāchóu* 发愁, and *zhāojí* 着急

Dānxīn 担心 and *fāchóu* 发愁 are interchangeable in meaning "to worry about . . . ," but *dānxīn* 担心 is more formal and conveys a deeper sense of concern than *fāchóu* 发愁, which is just used in the spoken language:

> You don't need to be worried about this matter.
> *Nǐ búyào wèi zhèijian shì dānxīn.*
> 你不要为这件事担心。

OR:

> *Nǐ búyào wèi zhèijian shì fāchóu.*
> 你不要为这件事发愁。

Cāoxīn 操心 conveys a really deep sense of worry, but is used colloquially and only refers to worry over one's loved ones, etc., and never over things like national or international affairs/ problems:

> Parents are always deeply worried about their children.
> *Fùmǔ zǒngshì wèi háizi cāoxīn.*
> 父母总是为孩子操心。

NOTE: Children, even adult children, cannot be said to *cāoxīn fùmǔ* 操心父母.

Zhāojí 着急 is to worry in the sense of "to feel anxious about" or "nervous about" something. It implies that the worry is outwardly apparent from a person's expression:

> Your car's broken down? Don't worry, I'll help you fix it.
> *Nǐ de chēzi huài le ma? Bié zhāojí, wǒ bāng nǐ xiūlǐ.*
> 你的车子坏了吗？别着急，我帮你修理。

(15) "To help": *bāng* 帮, *bāngzhù* 帮助, and *bāngmáng* 帮忙

As verbs, *bāng* 帮 and *bāngzhù* 帮助 are interchangeable:

> Please help me move.
> *Qǐng nǐ bāng wǒ bānjiā.*
> 请你帮我搬家。

OR:

> *Qǐng nǐ bāngzhù wǒ bānjiā.*
> 请你帮助我搬家。

BUT, *bāngzhù* can also be a noun:

> He gave me a lot of help.
> *Tā gěi le wǒ hěn duō bāngzhù.*
> 他给了我很多帮助。

Here is the difference between *bāngzhù* 帮助 and *bāngmáng* 帮忙: *Bāngzhù* 帮助 is a compound verb. *Bāngmáng* 帮忙 is a verb-object compound and literally means "help (with a) favor." Therefore, the word order is different depending on which you use:

> Please help me.
> *Qǐng nǐ bāngzhù wǒ.*
> 请你帮助我 。

OR:

> *Qǐng nǐ bāng wǒ máng.*
> 请你帮我忙。

Bāngzhù 帮助 can also be a noun, but *bāngmáng* 帮忙 is only a verb:

He gave me a lot of help.
✔ CC: *Tā gěi le wǒ hěn duō bāngzhù.*
他给了我很多帮助。

✘ BC: *Tā gěi le wǒ hěn duō bāngmáng.*
他给了我很多帮忙。

(16) "To take": *ná* 拿 vs. *dài* 带 vs. *zuò* 坐 vs. *xuǎn* 选 vs. *pāizhào* 拍照

To say "take something away, to grab something," use *ná* 拿 :

I took a cookie.
Wǒ ná le yíkuài bǐnggān.
我拿了一块饼干。

To say "take something or someone to somewhere," use *dài* 带 :

Don't forget to take your passport!
Bié wàngle dài nǐde hùzhào!
别忘了带你的护照!

I took my book to class (the classroom).
Wǒ bǎ shū dàidao jiàoshì qù le.
我把书带到教室去了。

I carried my book to class (the classroom)
Wǒ bǎ shū nádao jiàoshì qù le.
我把书拿到教室去了。

I took my Mom to class.
Wǒ bǎ wǒ māma dàidao jiàoshì qù le.
我把我妈妈带到教室去了。

To say "take a means of transportation" (trains, planes, automobiles, etc.), use *zuò* 坐:

I took a train to Shanghai.
Wǒ zuò huǒchē dào Shànghǎi qù le.
我坐火车到上海去了。

To say "take a course in school," use *xuǎn* 选:

What courses did you take this semester?
Nǐ zhèige xuéqī xuǎn le shénme kè?
你这个学期选了什么课？

To say "take a photo," use *pāi* 拍:

I take a lot of photos when I travel.
Wǒ lǚyóu de shíhou pāi hěn duō zhàopiàn.
我旅游的时候拍很多照片。

(17) "To lose": *diū* 丢 vs. *shīqù* 失去 vs. *shū* 输 vs. *mílù* 迷路

To say "lose some concrete thing/object," use *diū* 丢:

I lost my wallet.
Wǒ diū le wǒde qiánbāo.
我丢了我的钱包。

NOTE: *Diū* 丢 is also used in the expression "to lose face" (embarrass oneself): *diūliǎn* 丢脸.

His son used some crude language in front of other people. He felt really embarrassed (felt he really "lost face").
Tāde érzi zài biérén de miànqián shuō le cūhuà, tā juéde hěn diūliǎn.
他的儿子在别人的面前说了粗话，他觉得很丢脸。

To lose something in a figurative sense, as in "to lose a friend" or "to lose an opportunity," use *shīqù* 失去:

> Don't lose that opportunity to go to China.
> *Bié shīqù nèige dào Zhōngguó qù de jīhuì.*
> 别失去那个到中国去的机会。

To say "lose at a game or contest" use *shū* 输:

> Did your team lose the game?
> *Nǐde qiúduì shū le nàchǎng bǐsài ma?*
> 你的球队输了那场比赛吗?

To say "lose one's way," i.e. "get lost," use *mílù* 迷路:

> Buy a map, or otherwise it'll be easy to get lost.
> *Mǎi yìzhāng dìtú, yàobùrán hěn róngyì mílù.*
> 买一张地图, 要不然很容易迷路。

(18) "Produce": the difference between *shēngchǎn* 生产, "to produce something concrete like coal, manufactured goods, etc.," and *chǎnshēng* 产生, "to produce something abstract, some phenomenon, like dissatisfaction, unrest, etc."

> That factory produces running shoes.
> *Nàjiā gōngchǎng shēngchǎn qiúxié.*
> 那家工厂生产球鞋。

> Eating too much fast food has produced (the phenomenon of) obesity among Chinese children.
> *Chī tàiduō de kuàicān chǎnshēng le Zhōngguó háizi fāpàng de xiànxiàng.*
> 吃太多的快餐产生了中国孩子发胖的现象。

(19) "To leave": *zǒu* 走 vs. *líkāi* 离开 vs. *liú* 留

To say "leave" in the sense of to go out or depart, and when
there is no direct object, use *zǒu* 走:

> She just left.
> *Tā gānggāng zǒu le.*
> 她刚刚走了。

To say "leave" when you talk of leaving a certain place, use *líkāi*
离开:

> She left Beijing last year.
> *Tā qùnián líkāi le Běijīng.*
> 她去年离开了北京。

> He was 18 (years old) when he left home.
> *Tā shíbāsuì de shíhou líkāi le jiā.*
> 他十八岁的时候离开了家。

To say "leave" a person or people, also use *líkāi* 离开:

> 20 years ago he left his wife and children, and went to
> Africa by himself.
> *Èrshí nián qián, tā líkāi le tāde qīzǐ hé háizi, yíge rén dào
> Fēizhōu qù le.*
> 二十年前，他离开了他的妻子和孩子，一个人到非洲
> 去了。

To say "leave" in the sense of to leave something somewhere,
use *liú* 留:

> If you leave your backpack here, then you can go in.
> *Rúguǒ nǐ bǎ nǐde bēibāo liúzài zhèilǐ, nǐ jiù kéyǐ jìnqu.*
> 如果你把你的背包留在这里，你就可以进去。

(20) "To see": *kàn* 看 vs. *kànjiàn/kàndào* 看见/看到 vs. *kànchūlái* 看出来 vs. *jiàn* 见 vs. *jiànmiàn* 见面 vs. *jiàndào* 见到 vs. *guānguāng* 观光 vs. *míngbái* 明白

This is a perfect example of how ambiguous verbs can be in English compared with Chinese, even though English is so much more precise and rich in synonyms when it comes to nouns and adjectives!

The word *kàn* 看 means "to see" only in the sense of to go visit family or friends, and must be preceded by the word "go" or "come":

> I want to go home to see my parents.
> *Wǒ xiǎng huíjiā qù kàn wǒde fùmǔ.*
> 我想回家去看我的父母。

To say "see" in the sense of to catch sight of someone, use *kànjiàn* 看见 or *kàndào* 看到:

> Yesterday I saw a cat in the park.
> *Wǒ zuótiān zài gōngyuánlǐ kànjiàn le (OR kàndào le) yìzhī māo.*
> 我昨天在公园里看见了（看到了）一只猫。

To say "see" in the sense of to perceive or discern something, use *kànchūlái* 看出来:

> I can see you're interested in Chinese.
> *Wǒ kàndechūlái nǐ duì Hànyǔ gǎn xìngqu.*
> 我看得出来你对汉语感兴趣。

To say "see" in the sense of to meet with someone, use *jiàn* 见, if speaking colloquially (informally):

He angrily said: "I want to see your manager!"

✔ CC: *Tā shēngqìde shuō: "Wǒ yào jiàn nǐde jīnglǐ!"*
他生气地说:"我要见你的经理!"

✖ BC: *Tā shēngqìde shuō: "Wǒ yào kàn nǐde jīnglǐ!"*
他生气地说:"我要看你的经理!"
(I want to look at your manager!)

To say "see" in the sense of to meet with someone when you have arranged to meet them beforehand, use *gēn* [someone] *jiànmiàn* 跟 . . . 见面:

Tomorrow evening I'm going to meet my friends at a Chinese restaurant.

✔ CC: *Míngtiān wǎnshàng wǒ huì zài Zhōngcānguǎn gēn wǒde péngyou jiànmiàn.*
明天晚上我会在中餐馆跟我的朋友见面。

✖ BC: *Míngtiān wǎnshàng wǒ huì zài Zhōngcānguǎn jiànmiàn wǒde péngyou.*
明天晚上我会在中餐馆见面我的朋友。

To say two people haven't "seen" each other in a while, simply use *méi jiànmiàn* 没见面:

We haven't seen each other for 20 years.
Wǒmen èrshínián méi jiànmiàn le.
我们二十年没见面了。

BUT if you say one person hasn't seen another person in a while, use *méi gēn* [someone] *jiànmiàn* 没跟 . . . 见面:

I haven't seen him for 20 years.

✔ CC: *Wǒ èrshínián méi gēn tā jiànmiàn le.*
我二十年没跟他见面了。

✖ BC: *Wǒ èrshínián méi kàn tā.*
我二十年没看他。

To say "see" in the sense of to meet when you have not made arrangements beforehand to meet them, use *jiàndào* 见到:

> Yesterday I saw (met) the new Chinese-language teacher.
> ✔ *CC: Zuótiān wǒ zài xuéxiào jiàndào le xīnde Hànyǔ lǎoshī.*
> 昨天我在学校见到了新的汉语老师。
>
> ✘ *BC: Zuótiān wǒ zài xuéxiào kàn le xīnde Hànyǔ lǎoshī.*
> 昨天我在学校看了新的汉语老师。

If you only saw the new Chinese teacher from afar, but didn't speak with him or her, use *kànjiàn* 看见 or *kàndào* 看到:

> *Zuótiān wǒ zài xuéxiào kànjiàn le (kàndào le) xīnde Hànyǔ lǎoshī.*
> 昨天我在学校看见了 (看到了) 新的汉语老师。

To say "see" a place in the sense of "to visit" or "see the sights," use *guānguāng* 观光:

> I've always wanted to (go) see the Great Wall.
> *Wǒ yìzhí xiǎng qù Chángchéng guānguāng.*
> 我一直想去长城观光。

To say "see" in the sense of "understand," use *míngbái* 明白:

> I can see what you mean.
> *Wǒ míngbái nǐde yìsi.*
> 我明白你的意思。

CHAPTER TWELVE

· ·

WORD-CHOICE ISSUES WITH ADVERBS

(1) "From": *cóng* 从 ... *dào* 到 vs. *lí* 离

To say from one place to another or from one time to another, use *cóng* 从 ... *dào* 到 :

> from America to China
> *cóng Měiguó dào Zhōngguó*
> 从美国到中国

> from 9:00 a.m. to 5:00 p.m.
> *Cóng shàngwǔ jiǔdiǎn zhōng dào xiàwǔ wǔdiǎn zhōng.*
> 从上午九点钟到下午五点钟

BUT, when talking about the distance between two places, "from" is *lí* 离 :

> The movie theater isn't far from the college.
> *Diànyǐngyuàn lí dàxué bùyuǎn.*
> 电影院离大学不远。

Beijing is 8,000 miles from Chicago.
Běijīng lí Zhījiāgē yǒu bāqiān yīnglǐ.
北京离芝加哥有八千英里。

THEREFORE:

My home is close to McDonald's.
Wǒ jiā lí Màidāngláo hěn jìn.
我家离麦当劳很近。

My home is far from McDonald's.
Wǒ jiā lí Màidāngláo hěn yuǎn.
我家离麦当劳很远。

BUT:

I drive from home to McDonald's.
Wǒ kāichē cóng wǒ jiā dào Màidāngláo qù.
我开车从我家到麦当劳去。

(2) The difference between the two ways to say "first": *xiān* 先 and *shǒuxiān* 首先

To say that somebody does one thing FIRST, then does another, *xiān* 先 is used for "first." *Xiān* 先 is used only before VERBS, and never before NOUNS:

I'll study first, then watch TV.
Wǒ huì xiān niànshū, zài kàn diànshì.
我会先念书，再看电视。

My father says to learn Chinese well first, and only then go to China to travel.
Wǒ fùqin shuō xiān xuéhǎo Hànyǔ, zài dào Zhōngguó qù lǚyóu.
我父亲说先学好汉语，再到中国去旅游。

Shǒuxiān 首先 can be used to set up a sequence of events, too, but it can stand alone, followed by a comma and then the entire sequence, as in:

> After I return home, first I do my homework, and then watch TV.
> *Huíjiā hòu, shǒuxiān, wǒ zuò zuòyè, zài kàn diànshì.*
> 回家后，首先，我做作业，再看电视。

OR:

> ✔ CC: *Huíjiā hòu, wǒ shǒuxiān zuò zuòyè, zài kàn diànshì.*
> 回家后，我首先做作业，再看电视。

> ✘ BC: *Huíjiā hòu, xiān wǒ zuò zuòyè, zài kàn diànshì.*
> 回家后，先我做作业，再看电视。

Shǒuxiān 首先 is also used to say "first of all" when giving reasons for something or when giving an explanation of something:

> First (of all), studying is more important than watching TV.
> *Shǒuxiān, niànshū bǐ kàn diànshì zhòngyào.*
> 首先,念书比看电视重要。

> First (of all), China is not as rich as the U.S.
> *Shǒuxiān, Zhōngguó méiyǒu Měiguó nàme fùyù.*
> 首先,中国没有美国那么富裕。

(3) How to translate "actually" depends on usage

Qíshí 其实, "actually," and *quèshí* 确实, "indeed," are used in positive statements:

That person is actually Japanese.
Nàge rén qíshí shì Rìběn rén.
那个人其实是日本人。

That person is indeed Japanese!
Nàge rén quèshí shì Rìběn rén.
那个人确实是日本人。

Bìng bù 并不 . . . , meaning "actually NOT" (contrary to expectations or a previous argument), is therefore always used in the negative:

That person is actually NOT Japanese, he's Chinese.
Nàge rén bìng búshì Rìběn rén, tā shì Zhōngguó rén.
那个人并不是日本人，他是中国人。

For the past tense, *bìng bù* . . . becomes *bìng méi(yǒu)* . . . for "actually didn't":

He stayed in Beijing for seven days, but he actually didn't even eat one meal of Chinese food!
Tā zài Běijīng zhùle qītiān, dànshi tā bìng méi(yǒu) chī yídùn Zhōngguó fàn!
他在北京住了七天，但是他并没 (有) 吃一顿中国饭。

(4) "Although": *suírán* . . . , *kěshi* . . . 虽然 . . . , 可是 . . . means "although . . . , but . . . "

In any sentence that begins with *suírán* 虽然, the second clause must start with *kěshì* 可是 or *dànshì* 但是:

Although I'm tired, (but) I don't want to go to bed.
Suírán wǒ lèile, kěshi (dànshi) wǒ búyào shàngchuáng.
虽然我累了，可是 (但是) 我不要上床。

NOTE: Adjective + *shì* 是 + adjective, *kěshi/dànshi* 可是/但是 .
. . (less formal than *suírán . . . kěshi . . .* 虽然 . . . , 可是 . . . and
generally limited to adjectives)

> Although that restaurant is expensive, (but) the food is
> delicious.
> *Nèige cānguǎn guì shì guì, kěshi (dànshi) cài hěn hǎochī.*
> 那个餐馆贵是贵，可是 (但是) 菜很好吃。

(5) "Almost" = *chàbùduō* 差不多 vs. *chàyìdiǎn* 差一点

The word "almost" in English is almost always translated as
chàbùduō 差不多. *Chàyìdiǎn* 差一点 is only used when something
unfortunate or undesirable ALMOST happened.

Chàbùduō 差不多, which means "almost" or "nearly" is often
used with *dōu* 都:

> I almost have one thousand dollars.
> *Wǒ chàbùduō yǒu yìqiān kuài qián.*
> 我差不多有一千块钱。

OR:

> *Wǒ yǒu chàbùduō yìqiān kuài qián.*
> 我有差不多一千块钱。

> Almost all my money is in the bank.
> *Wǒde qián chàbùduō dōu zài yínhánglǐ.*
> 我的钱差不多都在银行里。

Chàyìdiǎn 差一点, which means "almost" and "nearly," only
in the sense of "just about . . . [verb that describes something
undesirable]":

I almost lost one thousand dollars (but didn't in the end lose that money).
Wǒ chàyìdiǎn diū le yìqiān kuài qián.
我差一点丢了一千块钱。

I lost almost one thousand dollars (actually lost nearly one thousand dollars).
Wǒ chàbùduō diū le yìqiān kuài qián.
我差不多丢了一千块钱。

I almost couldn't find the bank!
✔ CC: *Wǒ chàyìdiǎn zhǎobudào nèige yínháng!*
我差一点找不到那个银行!

✘ BC: *Wǒ chàbùduō zhǎobudào nèige yínháng!*
我差不多找不到那个银行!

I was almost late.
✔ CC: *Wǒ chàyìdiǎn wǎn le.*
我差一点晚了。

✘ BC: *Wǒ chàbùduō wǎn le.*
我差不多晚了。

(6) *Cái* 才：three ways to say "unless . . . "; "only if . . . "

. . . *cái* . . . (..才 . . .):

I'll go only if you go.
Nǐ qù, wǒ cái qù.
你去，我才去。
Literally: You go, and only then will I go.

Chúfēi . . . , cái . . . = 除非 . . . , 才 . . .

> I won't go unless you go.
> *Chúfēi nǐ qù, wǒ cái qù.*
> 除非你去，我才去。
> Literally: Unless you go, only then will I go.

Zhǐ yǒu . . . cái néng . . . = 只有 . . . 才能 . . .

> I can only go if my parents give me the money.
> *Zhǐ yǒu wǒ fùmǔ gěi wǒ qián, wǒ cái néng qù.*
> 只有我父母给我钱，我才能去。

(7) "Every time": *měicì . . . de shíhou* 每次 . . . 的时候 vs. *měidāng/měiféng . . . de shíhou* 每当/每逢 . . . 时候

There are two ways to say "every time," depending on usage. The first is:

> *měicì . . . de shíhou*
> 每次 . . . 的时候

> Every time we go to Beijing we eat roast duck.
> ✔ CC: *Wǒmen měicì dào Běijīng qù de shíhou, jiù chī kǎoyā.*
> 我们每次到北京去的时候，就吃烤鸭。

> ✘ BC: *Wǒmen chī kǎoyā, měicì wǒmen qù Běijīng.*
> 我们吃烤鸭，每次我们去北京。
> (A literal translation.)

The second is:

> *měidāng/měiféng . . . de shíhou, . . . jiù . . .*
> 每当/每逢 . . . 的时候，. . . 就 . . .

OR:

měidāng/měiféng ... shí, ... jiù ... (formal, written way)
每当/每逢 ... 时,... 就 ...

A time word always directly follows *měidāng* 每当 or *měiféng* 每逢, and the second clause must include *jiù* 就:

Every time it's the weekend, we (then) go to the park.

✔ CC: *Měidāng/měiféng zhōumò (de shíhou), wǒmen jiù dào gōngyuán qù.*
每当/每逢周末 (的时候),我们就到公园去。

✘ BC: *Wǒmen qù gōngyuán měidāng/měiféng zhōumò.*
我们去公园每当/每逢周末。
Literally: We go to the park every time it's the weekend.

CHAPTER THIRTEEN

. . . .

LETTER WRITING: GREETINGS, SALUTATIONS,

AND FORMS OF ADDRESS

The word order of name and greeting is different in Chinese and English. This is true for greeting someone in person or in a letter:

> English: Hello, Miss Zhang.
> Chinese: Miss Zhang, hello.
> *Zhāng Xiǎojie, nǐ hǎo.*
> 张小姐，你好！

When writing to your own parents in Chinese (for most of you, this would only be when doing an assignment for class, of course!), it is not correct to address them as *fùmǔ* 父母, "parents," as in "Hello, parents," but rather as:

> Dad, Mom: hello!
> *Bàba, Māma: nǐmen hǎo.*
> 爸爸、妈妈：你们好。

NOTE: In Chinese a colon is used after the person or people being addressed, rather than a comma as in English!

The phrase "It was so nice to hear from you," so common at the beginning of a letter in English, is not used in Chinese. Instead, write:

> I was so happy to receive your letter.
> *Hěn gāoxìng shōudào nǐde láixìn.*
> 很高兴收到你的来信。

At the end of a letter it is incorrect to use *zàijiàn* 再见, because you aren't actually "seeing" or "meeting" the person face to face.

In English, many people are fond of ending their letter with the phrase "With love, . . . " It is incorrect grammatically to say in Chinese *gēn ài* 跟爱, since *gēn* 跟 is used only to connect two nouns. In any case, the Chinese do not end a letter with an expression using the word "love." After all, the word "love" (*ài* 爱) is used MUCH, MUCH less in Chinese than in English.

It is usual, instead, to end a letter to a close friend or family member with:

> Take care of yourself.
> *Duōduō bǎozhòng.*
> 多多保重。

A more formal letter simply ends with:

> Wish you well
> *Zhù hǎo*
> 祝好

NOTE that in both cases there is no comma after the closing words and they are followed by your name underneath.

Index of Headings

STONE
BRIDGE
PRESS

Other Titles of Interest
from Stone Bridge Press

*Chinese 24/7: Everyday Strategies for
Speaking and Understanding Mandarin*
Albert Wolfe
ISBN 978-1-933330-82-2

*China Survival Guide: How to Avoid Travel Troubles
and Mortifying Mishaps*
Larry and Qin Herzberg
ISBN 978-1-611720-10-5

Chinese Business Etiquette: The Practical Pocket Guide
Stefan H. Verstappen
ISBN 978-1-93333-63-1

*Chinese Proverbs and Popular Sayings: With Observations
on Culture and Language*
Qin Xue Herzberg and Larry Herzberg
ISBN: 978-1-933330-99-0

*Japanese the Manga Way: An Illustrated Guide
to Grammar and Structure*
Wayne P. Lammers
ISBN 978-1-880656-90-7

*Crazy for Kanji: A Student's Guide to the Wonderful
World of Japanese Characters*
Eve Kushner
ISBN 978-1-933330-20-4

Available at booksellers worldwide and online.